Business Analysis, Requirements, and Project Management

Business Analysis, Requirements, and Project Management

A Guide for Computing Students

Karl Cox

CRC Press
Taylor & Francis Group
Boca Raton London New York

CRC Press is an imprint of the
Taylor & Francis Group, an **informa** business
AN AUERBACH BOOK

First Edition published 2022
by CRC Press
6000 Broken Sound Parkway NW, Suite 300, Boca Raton, FL 33487-2742

and by CRC Press
2 Park Square, Milton Park, Abingdon, Oxon, OX14 4RN

© 2022 Taylor & Francis Group, LLC

CRC Press is an imprint of Taylor & Francis Group, LLC

ISBN: 978-1-032-10975-6 (hbk)
ISBN: 978-0-367-76684-9 (pbk)
ISBN: 978-1-003-16811-9 (ebk)

DOI: 10.1201/9781003168119

Typeset in Garamond
by SPi Technologies India Pvt Ltd (Straive)

Contents

Introduction

Sometimes I wonder whether there needs to be a stronger connection between requirements analysis and project management. It seems pointless to plan a project when little to nothing is known about the proposed product's requirements. It's not possible to immediately adopt Scrum or XP in these circumstances because agile projects still need a good understanding of the requirements. If you know very little about the requirements, you can't take an agile approach because this assumes a reasonable product backlog (a list of requirements) in order to hang a project off. To get a reasonable product backlog, you need to do some good requirements management work. You can't really take any software development lifecycle (SDLC) without enough requirements.

Having spent some time working as an IT management consultant, directing an IT management consulting company, inventing a software product and being development manager for said invention (in various releases), and teaching the topics of business strategy, business process management, requirements engineering (in combination you could call this 'business analysis' in industry language) and software project management, I realise that the heavyweight processes for project management and requirements management that I was used to don't really work at university level, to students new to computing, because to manage the heavyweight processes (whether it is full-blown agile, full-blown traditional management, full-blown requirements management) takes more time and scale than a university setting can give. Just giving students an introduction to agile management doesn't help much either because conceptually it can be difficult to grasp for students who don't have a background in SDLCs. Around the turn of the century, many universities decided to teach Java to first-year programmers as they shifted from procedural code such as C to the object-oriented paradigm. It was assumed the students would simply take to this new paradigm like ducks to water. But they didn't. Universities I worked in and had connections with found their students failing first-year Java in large numbers. The ability to conceptualise object-oriented principles and to then code them for first-year students was too great a leap because they were coming from a foundation of nothing. I have noticed, to my surprise, something similar in assuming students would take to Scrum or DSDM or any agile SDLC easily and naturally. They do not. It's a conceptual struggle. Agile – like Java – was built on the back of and as a consequence of not entirely happy-camper developers working in the old ways, knowing that many projects would fail. Without that underpinning of doing things in a procedural way, to expect students to think in an agile way very quickly didn't work half as well as I expected. Some have no problem and excel but a lot don't. It is so logical to follow a waterfall project lifecycle for novices to software development because it is prescriptive and formulaic. Even though it doesn't normally lead to good results in practice on a regular enough basis – projects fail a lot according to the statistics, of which more later – students can understand waterfall: *Do requirements, do design, do code, and then test what you have and hand it over to the customer*. What could possibly go wrong?

Well, in practice a lot! And often! As such, I pushed to introduce agile planning into my classes and moved away from traditional project planning. But there's where I noted the problem – even though a small percentage really get agile, the majority of students don't. They don't understand the lifecycle of an agile project but do sort of understand an SDLC that's waterfall. Even those students who want to adopt agile in their projects and group assignments tend to actually do the work in a waterfall way and try to fit an agile management approach around it later.

The Textbooks on Traditional Planning Didn't Help

I've looked at numerous examples of Gantt charts and it's a struggle to find much in textbooks that helps students with real examples. Most information available provides generic content for traditional planning.[1] Though it is really useful for students to know the elements of design and tools to apply, including programming languages, the question that sticks in my mind is, if you've got an experienced team, even slightly experienced, they will know what tools and models and programming languages to use and produce. First-time round for students this makes sense to show them that they should do requirements, do design, do programming and do testing (and break these into their constituent elements such as design entity relationship diagram, construct wireframes, create responsive designs) but after the first go shouldn't real requirements examples be used?

To me, it makes more sense to teach students a prescriptive approach to development primarily because they will see how things connect, at least in theory and to introduce an agile way towards the end of this. I had spent most of my practice time in traditional project management but once I leapt into agile, I loved it. I assumed that students would do the same but they didn't have the traditional planning exposure or experience. I found in practice that traditional plans were great to design a project outline or schema, well, ok, a plan!, but hopeless to follow. Going agile was to me a no-brainer. But to students it took a lot of brains to get their heads around. Some didn't get it at all because they did not have the experience and underpinning of traditional planning and all that waterfall brings or doesn't bring to the party. It makes sense, therefore, to present to students the best planning bits of both traditional and agile, to do as many companies still do, use a hybrid project management approach.

I've included business analysis techniques into the planning. Why? Well, many business analysts have to double up as project managers – and vice versa – so rather than get them to perform two full-blown disciplines erratically, why not get them to perform a hybrid subset of management and analysis more optimally? I cover a number of business analysis, requirements and management techniques but note openly that many other techniques in all three of the above areas are not included that could have been, or even substituted for what is here in this book. There's only so much I can present in one book but the major motivation for what I have put together is to give students enough understanding of the early lifecycle of projects. As we move seemingly inexorably towards a more automated and virtual world, it seems that the business side of technology doesn't get taught half as much as it should be on computer science degrees. So this book may be able to fill some gaps in student understanding.

That's a lot to take in so in short: this book proposes as a method for students to use in their work, and indeed, with the goal of providing something that is, for want of a better word, 'scalable' to real-world projects. I will do this through a real-world example and the book will also include questions and answers for students to test themselves. I also provide a more detailed case study.

The Role of the Analyst – Manager

It is difficult to come by outstanding project managers and business analysts who can also be excellent at the other role at the same time. Organisations seem to be combining these roles significantly more and agile approaches lend themselves to this concept. They do this by strongly binding requirements management with estimation and scheduling. The role demands historically that the analyst will perform the standard work of gathering and documenting requirements and then once a reasonable idea of the product requirements are in place, the analyst may then take on the role of project manager. Here is the lag: project management work has to wait until requirements work has at least done much of what it needs, if not all. If the requirements need to be structured into a contract, then that work must be done with legal advice, business management advice and the analyst working in liaison with the client. But part of the negotiation over contract revolves around schedule and cost. So the project management work needs a good look in, too. But if we are in a situation where the project manager isn't on the project at all – it's been decided the analyst needs to do the work of the manager – then that's a lot for the analyst to get into place. It is possible other managers are asked to fill in the gaps but the issue with this approach is that: (1) There is still no assigned manager, other than the analyst; (2) Commitment may be superficial because the external manager has little buy-in to the project. It's also the case that the proposed project could be in conflict with that manager's work or idea for a product line or even that the technologists required to build the product are already deployed on that manager's on-going projects, raising the risk of a clash of impartiality. If your team members are going to be pried away from you to work on something else, and you were asked to create the plan and work out a budget (only as far as the contract needed it to be done), would you risk losing some of your team? Or having budget taken from your allocation? Or draw up top-rate plans for a rotten egg product or product line?

What Is It That Students Need to Know in the Early Lifecycle to Get Them through Their Studies?

This depends on what the student is studying. If the student is studying computer science games then the early lifecycle may not be attractive at all. But the consideration for such students is that ultimately the student will go out into the world to work in this field on projects where there will be a project manager/business analyst or if lucky, both. Or if not-so-lucky, neither. At the other end of the spectrum are the business-focussed students studying information systems or business computing that will need a stronger grasp of the early lifecycle. Software engineering students are somewhere in the middle of the computing spectrum. Once graduated, they will be core to projects, answering to team leaders and managers, as they implement the requirements that analysts have gathered.

Whichever degree is selected, ultimately the student will find that their course demands groupwork to produce a software product. That groupwork will require some degree of management and some degree of analysis.

What's in This Book

You will be presented with an approach to analysis-management that scales the business perspective from the, what could be called, birds-eye view of the business proposal as a model, a business process view, then structuring the technical problem into a recognisable pattern with problem frames, creating a requirements table of enough depth to be useful to designers and coders, and identifying core transactions and modelling them as use cases. Linked to the analysis are three management tools: the product breakdown structure (PBS), the Gantt chart and a Kanban board. The PBS is derived in part from problem frames. The Gantt chart emerges from the PBS and ensures the key requirements are addressed by reference to use cases. A Kanban board is especially useful in what is called Task Driven Development, of which more later.

This is not meant to be just another textbook but more of an overarching guide for students. It is really for computing students only (encompassing business information and management systems through to digital media, software engineering, computer science and games development – if your course touches the areas discussed here).

Projects emerge from a business need. You have to do two big things before a project can begin: find out what you need to do (the requirements) and plan out how to do it. This book is a start for you to get going on your computing projects.

Technology Car Crash?

Before we begin, I think it important to make a very strong point about the direction that technology is currently heading. First, I believe in people over technology. Technology is a service provider not driver for how we live. At least, it shouldn't be. In this industry, though, you and I both run the risk of forgetting this. We have lost sight of the higher perspective that we need to see beyond the tiny bubble we occupy most of our working and leisure lives to think about how what we do affects the world about us. What I do affects you, and vice versa. There are two views, you might consider, on our understanding of life. The mechanistic view is currently dominant where we are all flukes of chance and without intelligence in our being; life is there for the taking and Darwinian survival of the fittest is the modus operandi of science. It's a view that thinks tinkering with the building blocks of life is good, has no side effects and no consequence other than technocratic companies becoming wealthier. Their belief structure: Effectively, we are born, we are used and we die. End of story. The excessive use of technology is of this view. The idea of transhumanism is driven by this viewpoint.

The other side of the coin is one in which life is energy. This is Einstein's view of the world. Energy never ceases. It takes the form of us (physically) and though we cannot see it (or most cannot), we are bioelectrical beings, that is beings of light or energy. This means that we function on certain elements of energy. We eat food which our bodies convert into energy. We do exercise to boost our long-term energy. We soak up sunlight and literally recharge our mitochondria (the batteries) of the cells of our body. For energy to be used effectively by us, created by us. For the most scientific view of the energy-view of life, Rupert Sheldrake is the place to start.[2]

Data is the currency of the knowledge age that we are purportedly entering. I have my doubts about whether the hype will match the reality, and to be quite frank, I hope it doesn't. The hype being: machine learning and artificial intelligence becoming the driving forces in decision-making. I can understand and recognise that data is key to help inform decision-making but I disagree that our lives need to have decisions made for us by algorithms. In life-critical systems, this is different. I do want an aeroplane to use live data to make appropriate decisions (so long as a pilot can override this if things go wrong). I don't see any gain in driverless cars – it's just a motorway pile-up waiting to happen. What exactly is the point of a driverless car? Are we deliberately deskilling ourselves? Then what pride will we take in our achievements? The Disney animation WALL-E comes to mind. We are at the point where technologists have so much sway in life that we have created a cult of technology. The tech-funded media has made idols out of the owners of the big tech companies. We are told: 'Science says…' Science is not God. Tech is not God. But we are told to have absolute faith in them. By doing so, we are making those companies richer and more powerful that we should ever permit.

We are bioelectrical beings[3] and we should be fully attuned to the planet we live on. Technology has its place, a vital place in life, but the small number of tech companies should not have total control of the planet we are on, or on our lives and our daily decision-making. We are in the beginnings of a digital age where we are at risk of becoming part of a dangerous usage of technology called the Internet of Things. I never really got my head around this concept because it makes no sense on so many levels:

1. Human intelligence. It's demonstrated that using pen and paper leads to higher grades and better short-term memory recall than using laptops and iPads and phones. There's nothing wrong with using technology but let's not become 100 per cent reliant on something that may not be the best tool to use all the time. By using pen and paper we are engaging more of our brain. By using screens, we are becoming less intelligent. Of course, what you are reading is typed on a computer – so don't think I am saying 'no tech'. I am not a Luddite!
2. Our scientific curiosity will be crushed by the instant feedback we could get from the IoT. For instance, being told immediately on our device that 'x' is a tree of type 'y' when we point our gadget at the tree will stop us in our traditional investigation of searching through an encyclopaedia to find the leaf shape and bark structure for ourselves. The process of the paper-based search – like in using the library on campus – teaches us the attributes of patience and persistence. Coupled with a deeper learning, there is no substitute for this. The IoT will effectively kill off this golden way to learn.
3. The mechanism by which data is communicated (microwave radiation) has never been proven safe. 5G[4] in particular has been demonstrated to be extremely unhealthy to cellular life (that's us), especially to foetuses and young children who have an immature immune system. The industry pushing 5G on to us have under oath stated they have not conducted a single safety study on 5G. It's radiation, folks, and I don't know about you, but I've always been taught: manmade radiation is not good for the health! And the evidence, which is out there, clearly demonstrates this. Though Dr Becker (see footnote 3) was talking about the same health problems in 1985, the world has fallen asleep to this as we have become heavily addicted to the instant, virtual world at our fingertips. A different way to communicate with devices is needed.

Councils have used and are using AI to determine who qualifies for welfare benefits. So many people – real people – are being left to fend for themselves when they clearly cannot because an algorithm, pre-programmed by someone who never met the claimant, is being used to make a decision on that claimant's life. It really is a case of 'The computer says "No"!' The algorithm cannot understand case-by-case exceptions. AI does not understand what it means to be human and it never will. AI has no soul, it does not feel. It doesn't even think. All it does it crunch data through different algorithms. Saying that, sometimes AI and machine learning have been used for good, such as in assisting in performing surgical procedures. The other side of the AI coin is robotics. Hospitals in the UK are now beginning to use machines to deliver drugs to patients in wards. Nurses are being phased out and even injured by the autonomous drug carts as they bash past medical staff.[5] Is this really a sensible use of technology? And does it bode well for driverless cars? How much does all that tech cost compared to employing one or two people? Hospital wards can be lonely places for patients. For a patient to talk with a person, even if only for a minute, makes all the difference in the world. Being friendly with people is a healing power all by itself because when you're happy, you're healthier than when you're not. Loneliness is the number one killer of people in the western world. Being alone, really alone, makes you sick. The thirst for technology may be making people sicker or prolonging stays in hospitals, too. We have lost our sense of humanity as we carry on engineering a fake, virtual world, because we are mindlessly throwing technology at so-called problems that don't need high-tech solutions. Just think on the massive increase in use of technology over the last two to three years alone. Can we really say that everything on the planet needs a high-tech solution?

I am not saying technology is of no value – you wouldn't be reading this book without it. Technology is extremely valuable but we've forgotten the real life about us, that we are a part of this planet, that we need face-to-face communication – without masks! and that we are destroying life just for the sake of so-called convenience of instant technology at our fingertips (5G!). We are co-inhabitants of this planet and we must realise that what we do affects everything on the planet. Let us move back from such high-risk technology and focus once again on good-use technology, safe-use technology (benign) and in helping reverse the damage we have done to the planet. We can still have fun, and we all like to have fun. It's better to have fun without causing anything else problems.

I absolutely had to write these words above otherwise I would not be true to myself. As the world faces a global technocratic *coup d'etat*, we must be aware that we are connected to this planet in ways in which technologists choose to ignore. The western approach to most things is to dissect and ignore those bits we throw aside (out of our blinkered sight), continually forgetting that we are all on this one planet together, connected together by our very existence together. The key fact that we are a part of nature,[6] not apart from it, should drive us forwards in our use of benign technology to make the world truly better. We can do this but we need to wake up to the fact that the path we are currently on is headed completely in the wrong direction.

How to Read This Book

The book is effectively in two parts, of which there is some interleaving. Part one addresses the business and requirements perspective. The second half integrates some core project management approaches, helping explain how both requirements and management are connected. The remainder of the book is appendices, the first of which presents my solutions to the exercises presented in chapters for you to do. The second appendix puts together much of the documentation for the case study into one place.

Limitations

The world of project management is vast and this book barely scratches it. The same can be said of business analysis and requirements analysis. This book barely scratches those worlds either. All the book intends to do is give you a reasonable introduction to some key modelling and planning tools for when you get to tackle student projects that need you to address business aspects and project management. The book is intended for students on computing degrees only. I don't target practitioners at all, at least not intentionally. Whoever reads it, I hope you find it useful.

Notes

1 Agile planning interestingly doesn't do this – plenty of agile texts give actual examples from actual projects!
2 Rupert Sheldrake (2009), *Morphic Resonance: The Nature of Formative Causation*, Park Street Press. The book was originally published in 1981 under the title, A New Science of Life. Nature magazine commented on the first edition: 'the best candidate for burning in many years'. Such a ridiculous reaction drew my attention. Professor Sheldrake, once a member of the Royal Society, describes how neo-Darwinian mechanistic science (which we see now primarily as microbiology) simply cannot explain life in terms of DNA, chance happenings and as analogous to a computer programme. The world is so different to this robotic, soulless view of life that Professor Sheldrake set out how to describe the biology of life through *resonance* and inheritance via such resonance. Darwin himself agrees with the inheritance of characteristics but could not explain how.
3 To really understand the nature of life as bio-electrical, read Dr Robert Becker's *The Body Electric*, published in 1985, and pay special attention to chapter 15 entitled after The Beatles's song *Maxwell's Silver Hammer*. Dr Becker (a medical doctor) explains how electromagnetic frequency radiation has an impact on our biology.

4 I recommend you go do your own research on this topic. A good book that includes much of the work Dr Becker found is written by a retired captain in the Canadian military, Jerry Flynn, *Hidden Dangers – 5G*, published in 2019. He is a retired electronic warfare specialist. I have had some communications with him and can corroborate just about everything he writes as true. All the science – in the public domain – backs up the fact that we need to find a different and safer means of wireless communication. Another great source can be found at www.naturalscience.org.

5 I'm not making this up – this is reported to me by family members who are in the medical profession.

6 Clemens Arvay (2018), *The Biophilia Effect: The Healing Bond Between Humans and Nature: A Scientific and Spiritual Exploration of the Healing Bond Between Humans and Nature*, Sounds True Publishers. This book demonstrates how being in forests and closer to nature helps us heal and be happier.

Chapter 1

Business Concept Models

The idea of a business concept model[1] is to provide a frame of reference and description of business structure and knowledge where like things are put together – a classification of business terms, products, services and so on. The business concept model is really important to enable all parties in an organisation to speak the same language. Yes, employees will speak the same language whilst working. I am not referring to whether they speak English or Chinese or French in the office. I am referring to the language and terminology they use to describe how their business works. This may sound somewhat trivial but the biggest issue I have experienced and researched is the inability of business and IT to communicate their meaning precisely enough to each other to have a well-aligned business. Failure to align the desires of the business with the products the IT department provides to support the business's strategic intent is a massive cause of IT project failure, and even business failure.[2]

Business speaks business language and IT speaks IT language – and never the twain shall meet. The problem with this is that IT systems get built that aren't really spot on to the needs of the business. Some aspects are but there will be some misunderstanding, so the product developed won't really solve the business problem in the eyes of the business people. This may sound a trivial issue and surely it is easy to get right? Not really. It is the case there are systems and apps built by a competent IT team that simply don't get used because they didn't align to what the business really needed. I was once asked by my manager: surely the problem isn't as banal as a communication problem? Yes, it actually is as banal. But solving communication problems is not easy. Typically, on a tech project, the first time any formal consideration of terminology occurs is in defining a data dictionary. But a data dictionary is a transformation problem (see Chapter 3 on problem frames): take a 'real world' conceptual idea like a 'Customer Record' and transform it into a structure that operates in a database, conforming to mathematical ideas like relational algebra and something called normalisation. This is all well and good for an IT system because the system is constrained by how it can be programmed. However, the real world does not operate like a computer programme. The real world is viewed differently by every single human being. And each is right in terms of what they see is to them, a truth. The concept of a business is housed within their heads and is simply moulded by some real things and how they fit together (a structure). If we wish to provide a structure of the real world on an IT system, we cannot start with a data model. Nor can we start with a conceptual model like an object or class model. Why? Because these are technology models and are constrained by how technology works.

Object models can look like concept models but are really conceptual. A conceptual model tends to be an idea of what a system may look like from a certain abstraction. A conceptual model alters the basic constructs of reality in order for the model to fit within the rules of its construction and semantics – and like it or not, these are near enough always from a computer-system perspective when we are talking about modelling with, for example, UML. One such classic conceptual model is the entity–relationship diagram (ERD). The ERD is a viewpoint of what a database could house in terms of data, tables and relationships. An ERD will follow a process of identifying things like primary and foreign keys, and a process of normalisation, leading to third-normal form. You'd then build another conceptual model, a data dictionary, to explain how the attributes of each entity should be handled by the computer programme.

Business concept models, on the other hand, are not IT-system conceptual. What's included is real: products, customers, real transaction records and so on. Conceptual models are abstractions because a real customer is you and me. We capture a real customer in a box in our concept model. Key is the fact that the language used to build and explain a business concept model is the language of business. A business concept model could be labelled a repository of business knowledge whose purpose is to promote a shared understanding of products, relationships, services and so on that an organisation offers customers and in how the business is structured.

Why Start Here?

This book is about technology, isn't it? About requirements analysis and project management? Yes, it is but requirements analysis begins in the business domain. The business drives the IT to produce products and services that support the business endeavours. So as a business analyst, you need to really understand business. Business concept models are as good a place as any to start, if not better than most I have seen. I wrote about strategic requirements analysis in another book[3] and that walked the reader through a process of how to organise and run interviews, how to analyse results and how to create business models: goal models and context models. I think it's really useful still because it addresses what a business is in business for (goals) and how it does it (context or structure). You could use all that material in conjunction with what you are reading here or instead of. But for shorter projects, goal-context modelling is lot of effort and it will eat into the time you have to build the right solution. Business concept models are different and faster. They focus on language and meaning.

The Basics of Business Concept Models

There are three main components of a business concept model:

1. Business rules
2. Definition of terms
3. Concept diagram

Before we begin, there is a massive amount more to business concept models and especially business rules. I recommend you check out the many websites, books and papers dedicated to business rules.[4]

Business rules have been around for a long time but they don't seem to get the same coverage as business requirements even though they are the rules within which business requirements operate so are key to the success of business requirements. It might be tempting to say that business rules are constraints or parameters upon which a business requirement is enabled. Falling outside of these parameters or constraints would indicate a failure or error in the business.

Why Bother with Business Concept Models?

Business models abound in research and practice. What should lie behind each one is the desire to present a 'picture' of how a business operates. With this picture, it should then be much easier for IT systems to be built that align well with the rules of engagement for the business. When these systems are built and are aligned, the business should function more successfully than before. When an opportunity emerges for a new product or service, the first step a business analyst should consider is creating a 'to be' list of business rules that the company desires to operate within. Accompanying the business rules is a definition of terms. This definition permits the business to explicitly state the meaning of each new (and pre-existing) term the business will use in conducting this new line of business. That terminology is vital for technologists in creating a system that really does do what the business needs. Supporting these is the business concept model diagram, a visualisation of the structure of the new business opportunity. From this structural diagram, we can conceive of how business processes are going to be affected and what kind of systems will need to be built to support the new opportunity.

If you take a look at the history of IT failure, you'll see time and again that misunderstood requirements are top or near the top of the list of failure points. One reason is that technologists – and I am one – tend to view the world as technical solutions: formal requirements, data structures and so on. But I've come to realise through my consulting experiences and research that this technical view of everything doesn't work if it has no business or real-world structure to work from. As such, I want to discuss it here as I know this will be important to anyone who wants to become a business analyst, a business process analyst, a requirements analyst or a project manager. Even programmers want to know about what a business really needs so it's valuable for them, too. Ultimately, it comes down to the question: who makes the decisions in a business? The business people or the IT people? It's the business people even if they are IT people! To be successful in your business, you need to wear a business hat even if you're at heart a database programmer.

Business Data or Database Data?

One the key things that requirements analysts need to concern themselves with is data. But often data needs to be extracted from requirements descriptions, from use cases or user stories. You will also have to draw an ERD. What is this specific type of data representation built upon? If you have no *business* concept model, understanding the data you need to put into a database to represent the business is going to be at best, a good guess. You might succeed to some degree but not all the way. A business concept model will help you ensure the data you need to capture will be correct.

Introducing the Case Study

This book follows a number of different examples from different cases but primarily focusses on one. Appendix 2 presents the case study documentation in one location and each chapter will consider the case study in part either through example or by presenting you with an exercise or two to try.

The Fizzit case (in the box below) has quite a lot of information though there is a great deal more I haven't discussed yet and some of which I will ask you to do. Before we get there, let's look at Fizzit's business in detail now.

The background paragraphs should speak for themselves. I genuinely think such contextual information is vital as it puts the business into sharp focus. Fizzit is similar to a number of companies that provide a value proposition to the general public in buying up their unwanted items. Fizzit is a subsidiary company of TWOO, which is a well-known online store selling second-hand books, CDs, DVDs and computer games. TWOO's biggest markets are Australia (because Amazon has not had a presence there until very recently) and now in China selling school textbooks written in English. TWOO has its own supply chain in which it collects its items from charity shops and pays 10 per cent of sales fee to the charity shops to incentivise them to be interested in collecting books for Fizzit rather than throwing them away. By recognising that many people have stacks of old books, CDs, DVDs and now computer games at home, TWOO created Fizzit to address this untapped supply line.

The case study presents the general idea for how the supply chain works. The Customer tells Fizzit of the items he or she wishes to sell. An offer is made for each item (the offer is actually from TWOO though the Customer does not know this) that TWOO thinks it can sell quickly. In other words, TWOO knows what is in high demand and will pay a little more for these items.

The business rules presented in the box are a subset of the complete business rules for Fizzit (they are labelled 'A' here because business rules are presented alphabetically). The goals that Fizzit wants to achieve have been discussed and even how their business will achieve those goals. However, there is no discussion of the parameters by which the business will operate. These are the business rules. In the boxed example, the rules provide explanation of 'the trade' – a customer selling items to Fizzit.

FIZZIT CASE STUDY OVERVIEW

Fizzit is a company that buys items: second-hand books, CDs, DVDs and computer games from the public via a website and then ships them to its parent company, The World of Online (TWOO). Fizzit's website works like this: a customer enters barcodes from the different items into the Fizzit site. If TWOO thinks it can sell the item, then it offers an amount of money for that item. The customer can decide to sell the item or not. Once the customer has agreed to sell their items, a trade is commenced. The customer must package up the agreed sales items and taken them to a drop-off location such as their nearest convenience store.

The items are collected from the drop-off locations once a week and centrally stored in a warehouse in southern England. Here they are checked for quality. Assuming good quality, Fizzit pays the customer the agreed amount TWOO has offered. If upon inspection in the warehouse some or all items are in such disrepair that they cannot be sold easily – in the opinion of Fizzit – then no payment is made to the customer for these specific items; the unsellable items are then recycled. A customer can be banned for a year from trading with Fizzit if there are three or more items that are recycled in a single trade.

All approved items are sent to TWOO. They then advertise the items for sale on their own e-commerce site into 30 different countries. The main purpose of Fizzit is to create a supply chain for TWOO, who have over a million items in their warehouse at any one time.

Business Rules (subset)
A. Trade rules (may need honing)

    A1. A trade can only occur when there is between minimum of ten (10) items and a maximum of 99 to be traded.

    A2. A trade can only occur when a value offered of £10 is reached.

    A3. A trade cannot occur if 10 items are presented but the value is below £10.

    A4. A trade is completed only when a customer is paid for valid items.

    A5. A trade cannot be cancelled once it has been submitted.

    A6. A trade must request a drop-off location.

    A7. A trade must include the Customer's bank account sort code and account number or PayPal address.

    A8. An item for a trade can only be identified by its barcode or ISBN.

    A9. The price offered for an item is determined by TWOO plus an additional 5% markup for Fizzit.

Business rules A1-A4 are presented in Figure 1.1 as a business concept model diagram. The figure shows Trade and Item are connected only in the sense that a trade must have between 10 and 100 items. The connecting line effectively denotes nothing more than a connection. It does not say when, necessarily. The text 'consists of ≥ 10 to <100' provides description of the relationship. The arrow indicates in which direction the relationship should be read: *A Trade consists of ≥10 to <100 Items.*

When we read business rule A2: *A trade can only occur when a value offered of £10 is reached* we might be tempted to extend the description in Figure 1.1 to simply say: *consists of ≥10 to <100 and > £10.* But this might be a little too much. To avoid this, we can indicate a unary verb arrangement (the verb phrase 'value offered greater than £10' denoted by the star) just for the trade itself. A unary verb concept is a bit weird, I hear you say. Yes, it is a bit too grammatical. All it means is that one thing has a constraint upon it. In this case, even if the trade does consist of the right number of items, the trade cannot occur unless the value offered by TWOO to the Customer for the items is greater than £10. In effect, this condition makes the trade become 'live'. This very neatly addresses two of the business rules A2 and A3. In consideration of the next business rule, A4, is our thinking correct? One thing can help here: a business concept model diagram shows structure of business concepts, not process. Inevitably, you can see implicit process or causality in the diagram. We do need to think about a Customer in our diagram so that's good. Is there a direct connection between a Customer and a Trade? Yes, there must be because the Customer starts the trade, so we can say the Customer conducts the trade. Is a payment a thing? Do we think we can include it beyond text? What does a payment really do?

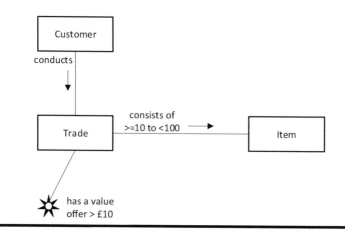

Figure 1.1 Business concept model for business rules A1–A4.

Shouldn't Fizzit pay the customer? Isn't the payment a point in time a bit like a state? What does it mean to have completed? When is the trade complete? Who says so? When is it official?

These questions bring into question the value of including this business rule into the diagram as it stands. I do not have a problem adding the relationship: customer conducts trade as shown in Figure 1.1.

When you think about the structure of the Fizzit business, it makes sense to include the Customer conducting a Trade. This is what actually happens. The Trade isn't completely in the hands of the Customer but it's fair to say that the Customer is the driver for the Trade. Without the Customer doing this, the business simply won't work.

This tells you something: the concept diagram does not need to include each and every business rule. The purpose of the diagram – in my view – is to present a perspective of what the business is. For Fizzit, the business is to supply TWOO with the right items. The mechanism for this is a trading shop window on the internet that allows the Customer to trade their items. The business is not about business rule A5 (even though this is important). For the Fizzit executive, they only care about how a Customer can sell items in the context of how they can fulfil their goal of creating that supply chain and do it all for a profit.

BUSINESS CONCEPT MODEL EXERCISE 1.

1. *Rewrite business rules A1 and A2 to not include amount values.*
2. *Draw a business concept diagram to match your rewritten business rules in (1).*

My answers (which are not necessarily better than yours!) are found in the Solutions Appendix 1.

The values presented above (≥10 and <100, > £10) are current values but these could change. What if Fizzit says reaching £10 takes too long for Customers (after a survey) and decides to reduce the offer value to £5? Does this invalidate the business rule above? No, but it would be better to describe a less changeable value rule. Why don't you try?

Business rule A4 could be rewritten: *Fizzit pays Customer on completion of the trade the completed trade value amount.*

Note that this value amount has become a noun concept and is modelled in Figure 1.2:

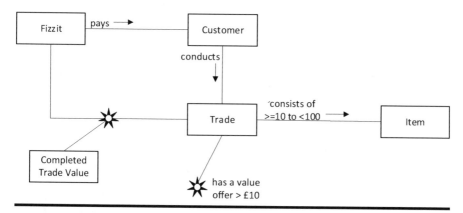

Figure 1.2   Completed trade value.

The star or sun symbol here shows that this particular connection between Fizzit and Trade is about the Completed Trade Value. I attach it to the connection and if there were no value available, the connection would not be there.

I don't think it is worth modelling A5: A trade cannot be cancelled once it is submitted. The diagram depicts what can be done and to work out how to diagram what cannot be permitted seems a little too much. I would suggest that when you arrive at such situations, you don't need to consider it in the diagram. I would even ask: is this business rule precise enough? At which point is a trade termed submitted? We need to think more about the business process, which is out of scope right now, but definitely in scope in the next chapter. But to just leap ahead briefly so we can answer the question: At which point is a trade considered submitted and non-cancellable? It is actually at the point beyond the next business rule A6 where we introduce a drop-off location. This is a place where a Customer takes their trade items for collection by Fizzit. Once the items are stored at the drop-off location, the trade cannot be cancelled. This then is a much clearer description for a business rule.

Business Rule 5 should be re-written: *A trade cannot be cancelled once items are stored at a drop-off location.* So, we need to introduce a new noun concept *drop-off location* into the diagram as shown in Figure 1.3.

In creating this figure, two things might draw your attention. The first one is that the star symbol is no longer on the value offer made in connection to the Trade. I've just written: value offer > £10. The second is to do with whether we are thinking of noun concepts around 'value'. The figure shows 'value offer' in relation to trade and a box with Completed

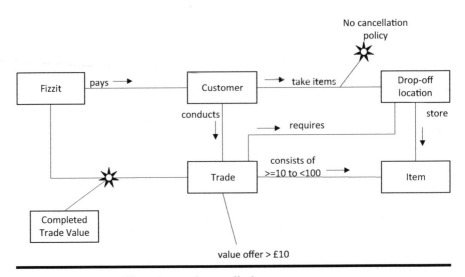

Figure 1.3   Drop-off location and cancellation.

Trade Value as the activator of the connection between Fizzit and Trade. Is a value offer the same as a Completed Trade Value? If it is, then why is it not in a box? But is it? To be frank, it's a decision you need to discuss with your client. I would not want to think about this in terms of a database identifier because we are not in that realm. I leave it to you. It is possible to improve the model. What is required is some clarity on definitions. More on this later but for now, let's continue.

The star symbol is now on the cancellation between the Customer and the Drop-off Location. I've added a word here: policy. I think the decision on whether cancellations can occur must be enshrined in policy so that there is consistency in operation of the business. I don't need to include policy in the business rule because the rule *is* the policy.

Business rule A6 connects the drop-off location to a trade but as we have already introduced the drop-off location in the diagram, I would recommend we switch rules A5 and A6 around.

This introduces another idea for you: the possibility of multiple lines between the boxes. In other words, multiple relationships between business objects (not in the sense of object-oriented objects). In Figure 1.4 you can see what I mean. When creating an account, we could designate the role of [registrant] to the Customer.

A business knowledge blueprint contains more than the diagram and we will get to the rest of it soon. Let's go back to the business rules. A7 states that a trade must include the Customer's bank account or a PayPal account (which is an email). Should we depict these in the diagram? I might be tempted to include something along the lines of Figure 1.5.

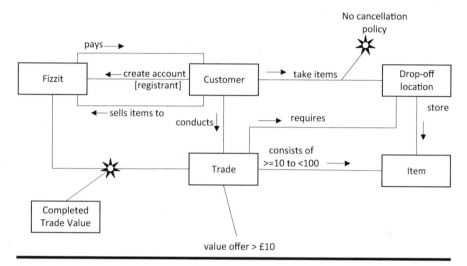

Figure 1.4   Customer at centre of concept model.

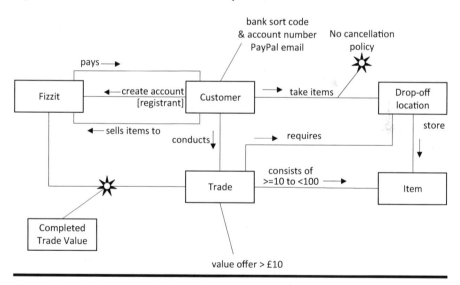

Figure 1.5   Bank account information.

I include the email because even though this is also most likely the email the Customer uses as a registrant, it might not be. We need to meet the business rule. I did not really want to create another noun concept in the business model because it is reasonable to assume that a Customer needs to have a bank account or PayPal account and these of themselves are beyond the control of Fizzit. We just show that this information is important enough to include in a business rule.

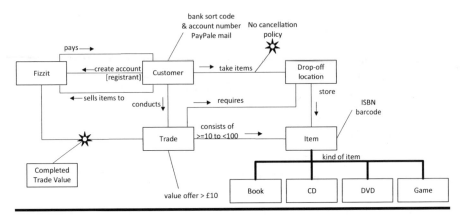

Figure 1.6   Item generalisation – specialisation.

The next business rule, A8, states that items are identified in a trade only by the barcode, which is the same as an ISBN on books but in barcode format to make it easier to track books through the processes of supply and purchase. Some books have two barcodes (ISBN and a shorter barcode to include more information, normally the recommended retail price). Does a DVD have the same set up? Yes, so do CDs and games. But the barcode number for a CD, DVD and game is a bit different to what an ISBN means. As such, we need to include both. I also wonder if we need to distinguish between the items in any way? You can see this in Figure 1.6.

There is the concept of generalisation – specialisation, as denoted by the thicker line hierarchy. We can see that Book, CD, DVD and Game are specialisations of Item. In other words, Item is a general thing and Book, CD, DVD and Game are everything an Item is plus more. I put on the hierarchy, *kind of item*. We also see barcode and ISBN linked to the Item. Let's assume the link is correct but is the hierarchy? Having spent a lot of time in requirements analysis work, hierarchy is a common concept. For the business concept model, it is the same concept. The issue I have with this specific hierarchy is what exactly distinguishes an Item from a Book other than the name? Is there a better way to list types of items? I think, in this case, there is. Don't get me wrong, you can use hierarchy if you wish. The standard Business Rules Group example uses hierarchy to distinguish between types of rental charge for a car rental firm. I can see in that case the distinction is greater than in our example. I would prefer to use a different notation to express that items can be books, CDs, DVDs and games. Figure 1.7 provides an example.

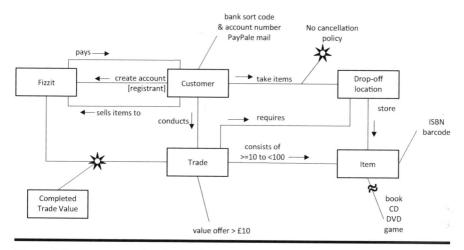

Figure 1.7   Item types: book, CD, DVD, game.

We can see that instead of a hierarchy, we have a double squiggly line and this symbol means that there are different types of item, specifically book, CD, DVD and game. This is my preference but if you think hierarchy as in Figure 1.6 suits your example better than go with what works for you.

The final business rule, A9, introduces a new noun. This is the organisation, TWOO, the recipient of the supply chain of items created by Fizzit. The specific business rule refers to a price offered for an item, plus a markup for Fizzit to allow them to cover their costs. See Figure 1.8.

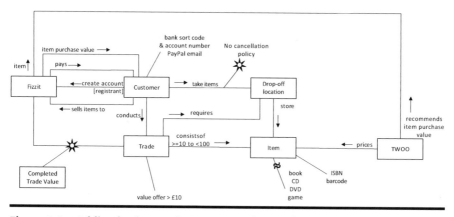

Figure 1.8   Adding business rule A9: TWOO item valuation.

We can see TWOO is added to the figure. TWOO prices each item offered to it via Fizzit. Also, we see an additional connection between Fizzit and Customer where Fizzit offer the purchase value of the item to the Customer. If TWOO does not want the item, then that value will be zero. Otherwise, the value offered by Fizzit will include a 5 per cent mark up as recommended by TWOO.

Revisiting Business Rules for Trade. Revised rules are *italicised.*

A1. A trade can only occur when there is between minimum of ten (10) items and a maximum of 99 to be traded.

A2. A trade can only occur when a value offered of £10 is reached.

A3. A trade cannot occur if 10 items are presented but the value is below £10.

A4. *Fizzit pays Customer on completion of the trade the completed trade value amount.*

A5. *A trade must request a drop-off location.*

A6. *A trade cannot be cancelled once items are stored at a drop-off location.*

A7. A trade must include the Customer's bank account sort code and account number or PayPal address.

A8. An item for a trade can only be identified by its barcode or ISBN.

A9. The price offered for an item is determined by TWOO plus an additional 5% markup for Fizzit.

Now that we've gone through the process of describing business rules and diagramming them, you can see a revised set of business rules. We've made a few modifications. This is a normal process of clarification.

Extending the business concept model beyond the rules and diagram to become a business knowledge blueprint means we need to define our terms.

Definition of Terms

Table 1.1 lists the terms that are of relevance to the business concept model we have been working through.

Table 1.1 Definition of Terms for Business Rules A1–A9 Regarding the Trade (see Figure 1.8)

Term	Definition	Example/Details
Trade	Act or process of buying or selling **items**.	
Item	A book, CD, DVD or computer console game (disc or cartridge version only).	Game consoles supported: Xbox 360 to current; PlayStation 3 to current.
Drop-off location	A storage facility where **customers** take their **items** for collection by Fizzit.	Examples: convenience stores (e.g. Martins), Tesco mini-store, Sainsbury mini-store. There are many other independent stores also acting as drop-off locations.
Customer	A person who is in the process of conducting a **trade**.	
Registrant	A person who has completed the Fizzit online registration. A registrant has not started the process of a **trade**. A registrant has never conducted a trade.	A registrant who commences a **trade** for the first time is designated as a **Customer** (and is no longer a registrant).
Offer price	The amount of money (in Sterling) that TWOO offers to pay for each **item** the **Customer** wishes to sell. Fizzit adds a 5% markup.	The Customer wants to sell her copy of *Harry Potter and the Philosopher's Stone*; an offer price will be made by TWOO to purchase this book, if and only if TWOO wants to on-sell the book.
Trade Value Amount	The amount of the **trade** minus the value of the offer price(s) made on **damaged item(s)**.	Fizzit offers a Customer a total trade offer value of £17.58 for 13 books. Upon QA inspection, one book is found to be damaged. Fizzit's offer value for this item was £1.12. This amount is subtracted from the original trade offer value: £17.58 - £1.12 = £16.46. The Customer is paid £16.46 in the transaction.
Customer payment	Funds transferred from Fizzit to the **Customer's** account.	

The purpose of the definition of terms is to ensure that the meaning of things is clear and that this knowledge is available to the business. It means that a customer cannot be anything but as the definition determines. It may be possible to be more than one thing, as expressed by the registrant. You need to have the definition even before you have the diagram. It's possible to have a clear enough understanding with the definition and business rules that you may not need the diagram. But I suggest the expended effort in drawing the diagram is well worth it because you can really begin to understand the rules and how the business works structurally. I use the term structure throughout because a business concept diagram's purpose is to express structure, not process. As such, you can start reading the diagram anywhere and it should make sense: just follow the lines. Use the definition of terms and the business rules to give deeper understanding.

Before we move on to the next chapter, I would like to ask you to attempt to create a business concept diagram and a definition of terms table for the following business rules, taken from the same case study.

BUSINESS CONCEPT MODEL EXERCISE 2

Here are the business rules for the drop-off location.

B. DROP-OFF LOCATION RULES

B1. The drop off location must be approved by Fizzit.

B2. The drop off location must directly link to Fizzit's system.

B3. The drop off location must provide adequate storage to hold the Customer's items.

B4. The drop off location must inform Fizzit of the arrival of the Customer's items.

B5. The drop off location manager should assist the courier in collecting the Customer's items.

For you to do:

1. *Create a business concept model diagram for the drop-off location.*

2. *Table any definition of terms that relate to the drop-off location business rules.*

You can find my answers in the Solutions Appendix 1.

Notes

1 Ronald G Ross (2020), *Business Knowledge Blueprints*, Business Rules Solutions LLC. Ron Ross has pioneered business rules analysis and business concept models for some time. He has built his work on decades of practical experience. I recommend you read his excellent book because this chapter is an introduction only. I can't go into the depth that Ron Ross does because he says it so well already. I am inevitably putting a little of my own spin on the approach because I am interpreting Ross's writing. In fact, I have a *concept model* in my mind of how to build the best business knowledge blueprints. I need to describe what I mean by a concept model and all its components in this chapter. I hope it keeps true to Ron Ross's work.

2 Probably one of the best places to start in understanding the quagmire of business-IT strategic alignment and a good (though complex) solution is the PhD thesis of Steven Bleistein who was my PhD student. Steve came from a business career having experienced a disastrous business-IT misalignment first hand at Bertelsmann (who tried to rival Amazon.com but failed miserably). Steve addressed the problem using strategy modelling and business process alignment. His thesis, completed in 2006, *B-SCP: an integrated approach for validating alignment of organizational IT requirements with competitive business strategy* can be downloaded from the University of New South Wales for free here: https://www.unsworks.unsw.edu.au/primo-explore/fulldisplay/unsworks_2117/UNSWORKS. Steve is now a highly successful businessman in Japan.

3 Karl Cox (2015), *Strategic Requirements Analysis*, Routledge.

4 Here are some websites relating to business rules: http://www.brcommunity.com/index.php; https://www.brsolutions.com/; http://www.ronross.info/; http://www.businessrulesgroup.org/theBRG.htm; http://www.businessrulesgroup.org/bmm/BRG-BMM.pdf

Chapter 2

Business Process Modelling

Following on from business concept models, we still need to hang around the world of business before we go into the software side of things. For those students who are asking, 'why are we doing this?' I thought I should write a few lines of explanation. The goal of many systems is to help improve a business function or purpose. We looked at how businesses function in terms of structure in the previous chapter but to recap here. That function could be how a department operates by introducing some new software tool to use in, for instance, increasing efficiency in filing, retrieving and editing customer orders. A structural diagram works well but it doesn't give us enough detail to say what happens first, second, third and so on. So, it's a good idea to draw a picture of how that process is currently working, then change the picture to make it look like how you would want it to work with the new software tool. That new picture is called a 'to-be' process model – if you produce a process model. You could use a rich picture from Peter Checkland's Soft Systems Methodology,[1] which is 'old' but still valid. You could draw a flow chart. Or a workflow model. A workflow is a bit of a process model explained in a lot more detail. I like rich pictures but those of us who do are receding in number as we get older and more tech-facing modelling tools emerge. BPMN, the Business Process Modelling Notation,[2] is current, popular and suited to the task. I like to use tools that are suited to the task. My advice is to look at the tools you have

DOI: 10.1201/9781003168119-2

good working knowledge of and think of them as tools residing in your toolbox. When you need to fix or make something around the house, you look for the appropriate tool; a hammer is good for bashing and even breaking stuff, but not the best for sawing a block of wood in two.

When there is an opportunity to describe how a current process in a business works, or how a new version might work, in relation to software – and sometimes not – then select BPMN out of your toolbox. You could pick Role Activity Diagrams (RADs),[3] which are excellent but not as popular as they used to be, or UML's Activity Diagrams,[4] which might be popular but not so easy to understand or draw. These choices are fine but your audience may not get it so readily with UML or your developers may not know of RADs. Something in between easy to follow and well known is the Business Process Modelling Notation (BPMN from now on).

BPMN was designed with systems in mind, in fact with automation in mind. Hence, you can get into BPEL, which is an executable language for processes used especially for service-oriented architecture. But we won't go there and we won't be discussed BPEL at all in this book. There is a slight kickback though in that the focus on executable processes has led to an explosion in diagram elements. There are a great many BPMN modelling elements to choose from. This is beneficial in that almost every conceivable scenario can be modelled. But the drawback is that it's more likely that you only need a small sub-set of the notation and picking the right elements from a long list can lead to mistakes. If you want evidence of how many elements there are, just look at the three BPMN stencils (at time of writing) in the excellent *diagrams.net*, the free drawing tool I used to draw the BPMN models in this chapter. There are over 175 different modelling elements available! This, in my view, is a little excessive for *business* process modelling but in terms of modelling how code might work (BPEL) then I think it makes sense. However, for our purposes, we don't need such an extensive knowledge. All we need is to understand a subset of the BPMN notation.

BPMN: A Very Useful Subset for Whilst at University

This section presents the most important modelling elements you will need to know about whilst studying. You may wish to learn more about BPMN and expand your horizons beyond what is presented here. Also, depending on where you end up in practice, as a business process analyst or programmer, you will need to add to your repertoire. But there are too many elements to cover in this introduction and the differences between them will be confusing at first. So, for now, let's look at what

I consider a very useful subset of BPMN diagram elements. After this, I will present a BPMN model for our case study.

Activities and Pools/Swimlanes – What Happens Where

Activities show what happens in a process. I tend to think of what before who so I suggest you start what actions occur in a process. You can then add context such as companies, departments, individuals, systems described in *pools* and *swimlanes*. Activities are what happens in a process but there needs to an indication of where the process starts and finishes. These start/stop actions are drawn as circles. Between circles are the activities, drawn as rounded rectangles. Figure 2.1 gives an example.

The start circle is on the left and the process is drawn left to right. There are two activities: Select products to order, followed by Submit order with payment details, and then the Stop circle, which is a thicker line than the start. All of this is wrapped up inside a pool box called Customer. The pool is the role or party responsible for the actions in the process. Figure 2.1 presents a pool – a single role that is separate from others. If there are several roles working in unison, for instance, different departments within the same company fulfilling a process, then you add swimlanes within the pool. Each swimlane represents a role within the collective pool.

Before we look at how we can communicate among swimlanes and pools, how a process may operate together to succeed – called orchestration – there is something about the activities we can add as extra information. This is called assigning a type to an activity. The first activity in Figure 2.1 could be done manually by the Customer flipping through a catalogue or in a store looking at items on a shelf. Or it could be done electronically via a web browser. These activities, which we can call tasks, can have a label attached to them to give us a better idea how that specific task is fulfilled. Figure 2.2 presents the types that are most common.

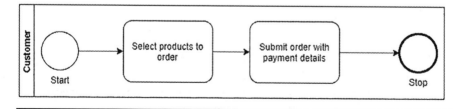

Figure 2.1   The customer process.

Type	Explanation
Task	None-specific action
User	At the interface of system
Manual	Purely physical action with no computer
Business Rule	Action must implement agreed business rule
Service	Function provided by a system
Script	Run specific code segment
Send	Message to external role (out of pool)
Sub-process	Abstract-out complexity (and need to describe it elsewhere)
Loop	Repeat this step a stated amount of times
Loop sub-process	Repeat this set of steps several amounts of times. Note that a loop should have a text note attached to explain what happens here.

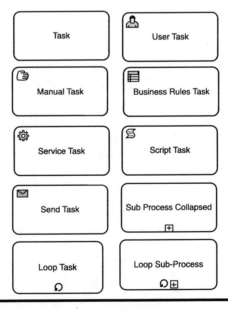

Figure 2.2 Task types (as defined in the table).

To elaborate upon the task types, where there is no symbol in the top left corner, this simply means we haven't allocated a type because we either don't know or it doesn't matter. Where there is a person (user) this implies anyone using a computer to fulfil their task. The hand means an entirely manual activity, such as taking a package in a warehouse and placing it *ex-factory* (outside the warehouse storage area) ready for collection and delivery elsewhere. A business rule is a requirement for a specific industry or company – we addressed these in Chapter 1. In our warehouse example, the task has to meet a business rule. For instance, the placing of the package to *ex-factory* may trigger a business rule to order new components to make another five products if there are now less than ten left in stock.

Figure 2.3 provides contextual examples. The top example shows a manual process (hand symbol) where the Customer selects products

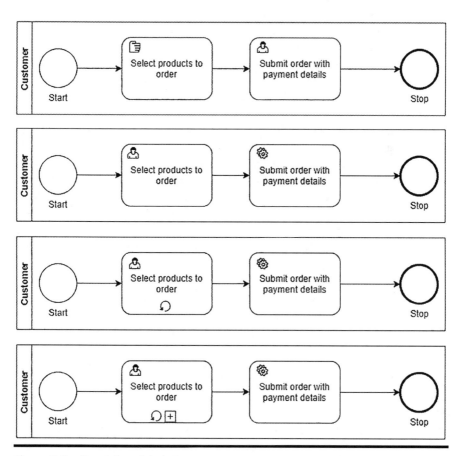

Figure 2.3   Examples of task types.

to order, for instance at a supermarket. The process continues with the Customer potentially checking out via a self-service till.

The second pool shows the first process as a user process. The Customer is likely selecting products online. The second task shows a cog-wheel indicating a service provided by a website, in this case the Customer places their order with payment. This process might be driven by a Customer that orders products via an online supermarket.

The third pool is the same except it contains a loop arrow in the first task. The loop indicates that the Customer completes this task several times before moving on to the next task. For example, a Customer could be selecting different books to purchase. Each one is added to the shopping cart, one by one.

The final pool in Figure 2.3 shows the sub-process 'cross'. The use of the sub-process symbol indicates that there are several steps that need performing in fine-grained detail and because of the loop, several times. For instance, the Customer in the sub-process might (1) Search for a book, (2) Read the reviews of the book. (3) Add the book to the basket. These three steps should be performed as many times as number of books are required. Loops should have a note attached to them to give the reader an explanation of how many loops are needed and whether there is a loop breaker to allow the next task to proceed.

Once you get to grips with these task types, you will understand that they are quite valuable in understanding where technology engages in a process. Not all processes will have tech in them but might want to have them. You can create a process model that explains the current situation which might be all or mostly manual and then another will show where potential changes occur where specific tasks are user-driven at the interface or are software services the new technology will provide. I tend to avoid the *script* type because it can be too close to the final software solution for the analyst to be concerned with it.

I will get to the important send and receive task types next but before that, I wanted to go over a basic core diagram element in process modelling: decisions and multi-threads. BPMN has an enormous amount of options for modelling decisions but for our purposes what matters is really two types: OR and AND. OR and AND gates are like logic gates. OR is simply a choice, for example, do 'a' or do 'b' depending upon the condition the process is currently in. AND is do both 'a' and 'b' asynchronously or in parallel. The 'condition' decision is known as a gateway in BPMN-parlance. This is a good term because in a process you will arrive at a gateway and subject to the type, you will go through the gate onto one path, the other or both. Figure 2.4 presents examples of both types of gateway discussed.

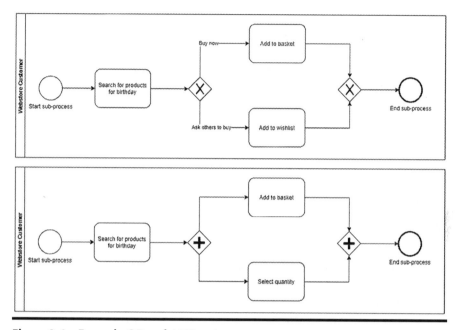

Figure 2.4 Example OR and AND gateways.

The OR gateway is the diamond with a cross in it. You don't need to include a diagonal cross i.e. the diamond can be blank but you do need to attach a conditional question to the figure. You can still include it with the cross. The AND gateway in the lower part of Figure 2.4 is depicted as a horizontal-vertical cross or 'plus sign'. It means both pathways are trodden at a similar time, if not entirely synchronously. We can do both Add to Basket and Select Quantity, whichever comes first. When an OR or AND gateway opens, it usually needs to close back to a single thread. We need to repeat the same gateway symbol and have both threads connect to it. Out of the 'join' gateway comes a single thread as we proceed along our process pathway. Sometimes you don't need to join back – it depends upon the process chunk being modelled.

Sending Messages

There are some very basic rules about how to communicate among swimlanes and pools that I have to question the realistic nature of. Namely, if you are in a pool of several swimlanes, you cannot send a message from one swimlane to another. So this means you cannot send an order for parts from a production line to the procurement department. Or at least you cannot use the message sending notation that is the obvious tool of choice. This often confuses students because it would be the clear choice of notation to indicate something important is being sent, like an attached parts order document in an email. But BPMN has a different take on messages and these are: you can only use the message symbol (task type) when sending a message out of one pool to another pool. Also, the receiving pool does not have to be modelled – and often we don't know how a different organisation functions so we cannot model it as it is – so the message arrow just has to go to the receiving pool edge. Figure 2.5 shows how messages can also trigger a process.

There are two pools depicted, both of one swimlane: the Customer and the Book Seller. The Customer selects books to order (a subprocess is indicated by the + sign thus taking more than one step). This is a looped subprocess also meaning it can be repeated many times. We don't need to describe it here. The Customer then submits the order – let's say it is an online form, like you may find on worldofbooks.com. The 'send' message is indicated by the dark envelope task type. A special message arrow is used: a dotted line with a triangular, white head. The Book Seller receives the message directly into a double circle start state, with a clear envelope in it. This start state symbolises that a process is now triggered by the incoming message. In other words, the process is dormant until it receives the trigger message containing the book order. The Book Seller processes the order on its system; there is an AND gate post this. The AND (diamond with big + sign) indicates that both threads are activated. It is asynchronous meaning either one can finish before the other. We separate the steps because they would be managed by different departments in the Book Seller company. Prepare Shipment would be a warehouse or stockroom operation and I've labelled it as manual because overall it involves a member of staff locating the book(s) on shelves, placing them in an envelope or package and then placing that package in the postage area to be shipped. Manage Payment would

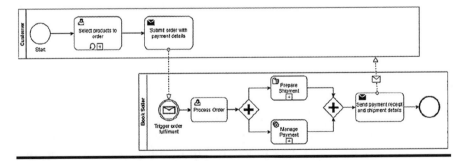

Figure 2.5   Messaging example in BPMN.

be a process for the Accounts Department or equivalent, and the steps there probably would mean updating the Customer account to link to the payment made, as well as processing the payment itself. I've labelled this a service task type assuming that overall the majority of this would be automated. Once both actions are complete the process joins back to a single thread. A message is then sent to the Customer (the outgoing message is a dark envelope task type) and a message arrow leaves the action and travels to the edge of the Customer pool. I don't need to show what the Customer does to receive the message as it is not important in modelling the process. All we need to know is that the message has been sent containing the relevant payment receipt and shipping information. The clear envelope on the message arrow is optional. You don't need to place it there. But it's fine to do so as it stands out as a message, be it email, text, instant chat, posted letter or whatever.

There are a great many variations when it comes to message sending and receiving. You will read about throwing and catching when it comes to messages and other aspects of BPMN I haven't covered here. This is programming-speak. Throw and catch are error-handling terminology in programming. I won't go into the details as it is something we should not need to think about at the business end of the project. But since one of the strengths of BPMN is in how it transitions to an executable language (BPEL), it is natural for programmers at this level to label things in programming-speak. I think it is useful for other aspects of modelling in BPMN but not really for messages. You send and receive a message, you throw and catch a ball. Irrespective of this, for you, it's fine to know this terminology and then to not worry about it again. For those who are interested in executable business process languages, throw and catch will really help you understand what's going on.

Data and Databases

In discussing programming, we conveniently move on to one more aspect of BPMN that is useful for us at the business analysis stage of the project, and that is how to describe data or documents in a process and where to include explicit references to databases. Figure 2.6 provides some examples of how to describe databases. Note that we have two swimlanes, Shipping and Stores, within a Pool labelled Book Seller.

Let's start with the data object 'Orders'. All we signify when we include data objects in a model is that there is a document or a record that we need to be conscious of. The dotted arrows just indicate what it is that is passed from one action to another. Mostly, we make an assumption about what passes between actions but we can make it explicit if we so wish. Datastores or databases are the barrels in the figure here labelled

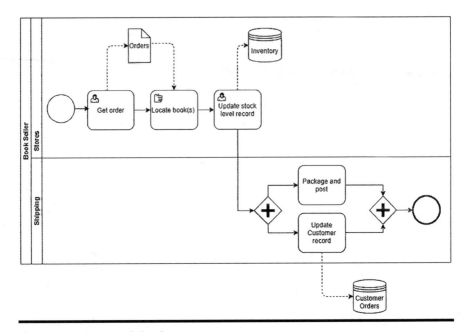

Figure 2.6   Data and databases.

'Inventory' and 'Customer Orders'. We can include a database within a swimlane as in the Stores swimlane because this database 'resides' in Stores and relates specifically to what is in stock. By 'reside' I am referring to ownership. Stores own the inventory so the database belongs to them. Where the server is physically housed does not matter for us in this context. Other departments would have direct access too, such as purchasing. The Shipping example is a little different because shipping updates the Customer record on the Customer Orders database. It is very likely that this database belongs elsewhere – it isn't the property of Shipping as the Inventory database is to Stores. It's more likely that Customer Orders would reside with a customer-facing department. The dotted arrow means we are accessing the database to update it.

BPMN EXERCISE 1

Answer the following question in producing the BPMN diagram for the following scenario. You'll find my version of an answer in Solutions Appendix 1.

You are a tourist who has booked a holiday to Beijing. As part of your journey, you book your stay in Hotel Hightech, the world's leading high technology hotel. Every room has voice activation to open-close room doors, curtains, switch on lights and the TV. The problem for you is that the voice activation only recognises Chinese. So you have to use the new voice feature on Google Translate that takes your typed in text, translates it and speaks it in your language of choice. Model your online booking process, your journey (by plane) and an experience of using voice activation in Hotel Hightech.

When I was really investigating business process modelling with a more commercial hat on, over 15 years ago now, with BPMN in its infancy, there were something like 200 business process standards in usage or proposed. It was a world of confusion. But in terms of industry, it was a rapidly growing area of importance for tool developers as increased automation and data management began to be viewed as business growth key factors. I was not too keen to move on to BPMN at the time because for me it appeared to be a modelling language that programmers liked; it was not designed with business in mind. BPMN was designed as a tool to aid process automation. As such, I kept to RADs because they were very business-focussed, they worked, they were easy to use and easy for clients to read, with a key supplied. Also, I just liked their flexibility. Lots of work had occurred at the University of Southampton to 'enact' the notation, meaning that it was possible to step through the process decisions and threads via an automated tool. Though this enaction was useful, it could not replace the models themselves. Enaction was a necessary step towards automation. I thought RADs had huge opportunities but, in the end, BPMN took over. Something was needed to rationalise the business process modelling, enaction and automation world, and BPMN was it.

BPMN has gone through some significant revisions and I won't bore you with the details. But I think it has become much more accessible at a business level than initially it appeared. I have grown to like it. BPMN does have some really curious aspects such as the hundreds of diagramming elements it contains in the specification – much of this is because of its automation origins.

Errors and Cancellations

One of the issues that business process modelling has had is capturing enough realism to go beyond the idealism that everything really works according to the diagram. To explain, an example:

You are in the middle of booking a holiday with a travel agent at the agent's office. You get to the point of selecting a hotel – having booked your flight already – and have gone through the process of confirming the hotel. At the point of which the agent has clicked 'Book', having already entered your credit card details, notices another hotel, with a better view and higher quality for the same price, has a room available. In fact, this was the hotel the customer had originally wanted to book. But the agent had made a mistake as the hotel names and location are near identical. An error has been made on the part of the agent and he has to undo some of the process. It may even be necessary to cancel the booking immediately (wait more than 24 hours and a cancellation cost will be imposed) and rebook the customer's original hotel correctly.

BPMN deals with such an example with its 'error' and 'cancel' events notation. I also think this fits with modelling *use case extension points* brilliantly but this is not for now. I will get to use cases later. But for now, let's take a quick look at the way BPMN models these. Figure 2.7 shows my attempt to model the scenario as if it works perfectly:

I haven't included a pool/swimlane in Figure 2.7 because I just wanted to clarify the core steps: (1) Find holiday; (2) Book flight (air ticket); (3) Book hotel. Assuming the customer is happy, then this process is fine. I've labelled find holiday a user task because I am assuming a travel agent is working at their computer to find the holiday. The bookings are services provided by the booking systems, so I've used the two cogs symbol task type.

Let's now look at error handling as BPMN does it. Figure 2.8 presents the idea of trying to reverse a hotel booking from the perspective of the agent. You will see that this is a little more complicated than the ideal process. I kept the ideal process really basic just to give you the idea. Each activity has a subprocess button so clearly there is much more to it, which is what we would expect. Anyway, back to the 'error' process. Let's talk our way through it.

First, we will start with the Agent pool. It is the travel agent who works through the process on his computer. The Agent has the customer

Figure 2.7   Ideal booking process.

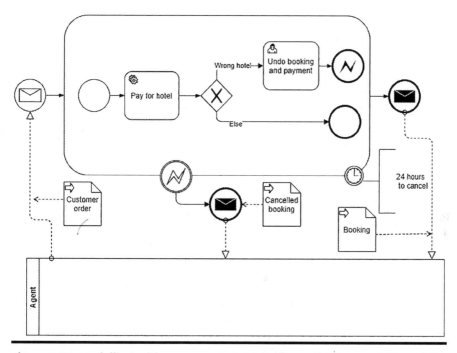

Figure 2.8 Modelling with error symbol. Note Figure 2.8 is a variation of the figure on page 212 of Kenneth J. Sherry's brilliant book on BPMN, *Complete BPMN Pocket Reference,* **Admaks Publishing, 2015.**

order (for the flight and hotel) and this triggers the subprocess above it. The subprocess commences with the hotel payment and then we find an OR gate. The upper choice is 'Wrong hotel' – the agent realises the mistake and then the action is to 'Undo booking and payment.' I've labelled this a user task since it was a human error that caused it. I have not labelled this with a subprocess '+' but I could have. Now once that action is done we move to the sideways 'Z' signifying the error and its correction have been addressed. The other choice is 'Else' which means in all other circumstances, we end the subprocess here. The outcome of the Else and finish of the subprocess (black line circle with dark envelope in it) means we have completed the Booking, which is sent to the Agent. So, the booking is sent to the Agent in the event that everything runs fine with the process and the hotel is booked successfully.

In the circumstance that the Wrong hotel has been selected and the undo has been enacted by the Agent, then we have what is called the 'Error boundary interrupting' symbol, the sideways 'Z' in the double-lined circle sitting on the border of the subprocess box. This is called into play in the event of the wrong hotel selection and the undo, as

I previously said. The result of the error boundary interruption is a message sent to the agent signifying the booking has been cancelled. Ironically, though this is labelled an error, it is in fact a success: the booking has successfully been cancelled. The error symbolism is more suited to programming than it is to a business process and I think that the symbol would be well-employed in this circumstance.

As I said, there is another option: cancel. It would also be possible to model this process with a cancel symbol and this may appear to make more sense. You replace the 'Z' in the error symbols with an 'X' to mean 'cancel'. Now this sort of makes sense to use: the agent wishes to cancel the transaction so the cancel symbol works. The process is exactly the same as in Figure 2.8. Make one change and that is to swap out the error 'Z' symbol for the 'X' cancel symbol. The question we need to ask is, does the cancel 'X' wipe out the process at this point and close down any other threads in the pipeline?

Probably it doesn't. When I speak the words 'cancel booking' then I think the 'X' works. Yet, I want to point out the mistake made and that it may be possible to resolve the mistake. So, in the end, I think the error 'Z' works best. However, it should be noted these symbols had the ease of programming in mind so error handling, in a programming sense, would seem the right choice. What I suggest for you is to think about the process in terms of its operation. Is it more strategic or more shop floor?

There is one more thing to mention – the clock symbol. This is a timer and it works as a constraint: the cancellation must complete within 24 hours of the original booking. The text is vital to explain the inclusion of a timer. There is a business rule for the travel agency industry and that is, if any booking is cancelled within 24 hours of booking, then no fines or cancellation fees are imposed. Please don't think this applies to the real travel agency industry. I am referring to the example only and I do so just to illustrate the clock event. The two-pronged text box next to the clock is a BPMN standard for placing text or notes on the diagram.

As I have said, to include all the notations and variations here would mean I need to write a whole book but there are books already out there that do this. All I want to show you is what I feel are the most useful *business* process elements of BPMN when you are studying for your computing degree. Before we move on to the next chapter, on problem frames, we need to explore whether there is any linkage between business concept models (Chapter 1) and business processes. In other words, are there things in a business concept model that might help us in determining what to put into a process model?

From Concept to Process

Ron Ross makes it very clear in his work on business knowledge blue-prints that a concept model diagram is not a process model, that you cannot effectively 'click' it and a process will enact. I agree with him that models should really only be read one way and only mean one thing. The purpose of the business concept model is to provide a structure for business understanding. The purpose of a business process model is to document repeatable actions across a business structure to provide understanding for how a wider transaction or business operation will work. Hence, we have the term 'enact'. My view is the same as Ross but on the other hand, I would like to know more about how I can get the business to work according to the business rules and the concept model diagram. That knowledge could be termed business process knowledge. So, though I agree that clicking a concept model element should not deliver you a process, you should still be able to reason about the concept diagram and infer aspects in it that could relate to a process. If we accept this as useful then there are a number of things to consider:

1. What things do we really need to know about in a process model?
2. Are these things in a concept model diagram?
3. Is a thing in a process model really the same as the thing (semantically, i.e. in meaning, not just in nomenclature) in the concept model diagram?

Let's answer these now. I will present answers in Table 2.1 and add any required explanation as needed.

I won't continue the table because you may see from the rationale that the business concept model and the business process model really are different things. The concept model I have which links the business process and concept diagram together is really all in my head. This is as Ron Ross explains with concept models – it's all in your head! The diagram, business rules and definitions are there to make some sense of what's in my head, or your head, as you look at these things. So, when I look at a concept model, I begin to fathom how a process model might work in parts of it. But explicitly describing what element matches another is very difficult.

Case Study: Fizzit in BPMN

In Chapter 1, we introduced the major case study in this book (though we recognised also myriad other examples would be used to give 1.

Table 2.1 Relating BPMN with Business Concept Models (BCM)

BPMN Element	BCM Diagram Equivalent (see Chapter 1)	Potential Match?	Rationale
Swimlane/pool	Entity (noun phrase)	Yes	Most boxes in the concept model relate to value chain elements such as the drop-off location, TWOO, Customer and so on. These are clear candidates for roles in a business process (modelled as pools and swimlanes).
Messages between pools	Active noun value associated between entities	Yes?	The star–sun symbol that sits on an association with a noun thing attached (as described in Chapter 1) represents an active or live connection where the noun box is the message that is passed in the BPMN model, either as an email, phone call, document, product or voice.
Action within one pool or swimlane	Association between entities	Cautious	In a concept model, these verb phrase relationships can suggest movement of e.g. documents or products but mostly they show how one thing is related to another. With caution because a business concept model is read both ways from thing to thing but a process only flows in one direction or down one (or several) thread(s).
OR gate	Condition on association	Yes?	An OR gate will check the condition placed on the gate to decide which thread to follow. Business concept models can provide such conditions but they don't provide, necessarily, an alternative option if the condition is not met. They also don't dictate what happens next when a condition is true, which is crucial for us to know in a process.

(Continued)

Table 2.1 (Continued) Relating BPMN with Business Concept Models (BCM)

BPMN Element	BCM Diagram Equivalent (see Chapter 1)	Potential Match?	Rationale
AND gate	—	None	We can speculate that the condition on an associate in a concept model may act like an AND gate. But for which thread? What happens next? All we see in a concept model is a connection between two noun phrases (let's call them things because noun phrase is really awkward). But we don't know much more than this.
—	Generalisation-specialisation	None	No element in BPMN even though there are subprocesses (and I presume we call higher abstraction processes *super* processes?).

Further clarity and 2. A different perspective). I am going to now present a business process model for Fizzit using BPMN. I won't model the whole process here, just a piece. The complete BPMN process model for Fizzit can be found in Appendix 2. If we look back to Chapter 1, you see I will work with the business rules around conducting a trade and focus on the first part of the process, the Customer using the Fizzit site to sell items (books, CDs, DVDs, games).

We can see two pools in Figure 2.9. One is the Customer (on top) with the Fizzit website below. Should we include a system here? I don't see why not. I think in this context it makes sense because the Customer needs to use the Fizzit website to create an account. You'll notice that there are effectively three separate processes included in the Customer. One is manual (denoted by the hand signal) and is for the Customer to *organise items to sell*. It's floating on its own because it is not certain when the Customer needs to do this. For instance, the Customer may have found the Fizzit site, signed up for an account and then organised books and so on to sell. But it may also be the case that the Customer did it the other way around. Because it doesn't matter, we have the action floating. The longer process within Customer contains two subprocesses. One is to *Add items to trade*, which has a repeat loop, meaning we do this subprocess multiple times until the condition is met (repeat until all

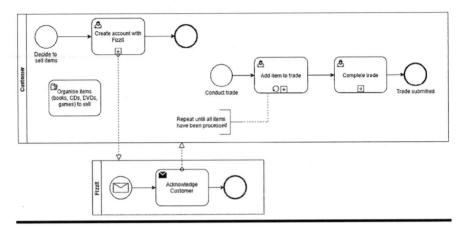

Figure 2.9   Fizzit customer trade process.

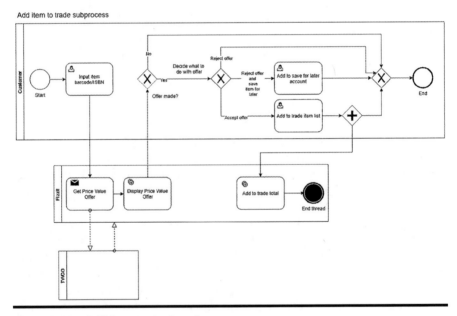

Figure 2.10   Add item to trade subprocess.

items submitted i.e. have gone through the process of being added to trade). Then the second subprocess occurs to *Complete trade*. This does not have a repeat loop so the whole subprocess should be run once through. Note that the subprocess can include a repeat loop step within it. The subprocess for *Add Item to Trade* can be seen in Figure 2.10.

There are three pools in this subprocess: Customer, Fizzit Website and TWOO. The Customer inputs a barcode or ISBN into the website, which triggers a message to be sent to TWOO to return a price value. Note that TWOO does not have any internal process steps defined. This is because TWOO is a separate business to Fizzit's and how it does its business is its concern, and out of our scope. Once a price has been offered, the Customer has to decide what to do with the offer. It can be rejected and then the process ends. Remember this is a subprocess that is repeated until all items have gone through it. An alternative outcome is that the Customer decides not to sell the item – so effectively rejects the price offered but places the item in a 'save for later' area. The idea is that when the Customer does decide to sell the item, there is no need to input the barcode again – just retrieve the item from the save for later space. This is beyond the scope of this subprocess example so we don't include that description here. The final option is for the Customer to add the item to the trade. The Fizzit website then adds the item to the prospective trade. The subprocess ends here and will be repeated until no items are left. Note that if no price is offered – TWOO may not require the item – then the subprocess ends for this item.

Note the 'script' task symbol for Check number of items and value of trade in Figure 2.11. The script means a function is called in the code of the system. Normally, you would be expected to provide the code as well as the model, but given we are interested in the *business* process, we'll leave the programming until a later date. It's important to use this

Complete trade subprocess

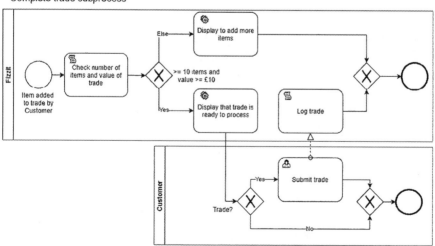

Figure 2.11   Complete trade subprocess.

symbol to flag that some codework has to be done. Beyond that, the business subprocess in Figure 2.11 will check that enough items and value is now reached in order to conduct a trade. If this is not the case, then the Customer is asked to add more items. We end the process here. If, however, there are more than ten items and with a value of greater than £10, then Fizzit (via its website) will ask the Customer whether to trade or not. The Customer can refuse – there may be more items – in which case the subprocess ends. Or the Customer may accept and Submit the trade. Fizzit then logs the trade (using a script) and the process ends.

One thing I haven't done is label anything in the business process model as 'website' or 'system'. There are reasons why: I want to keep technology agnostic even though it's pretty obvious the Customer would need to use the website application to input the barcodes or ISBNs of their items. I could have used website in the models but then there are times when the functionality to be expressed might not be a website but an application. Or it could be an underlying system or backend to the application. I think the chances of us knowing for certain which software application or system is going to be used for what action or activity – remembering we are business analysts and are discovering how the business would work in accordance with the business concept model and business rules – is unlikely. I would rather be more generic and talk about the business of Fizzit rather than the technology it has yet to build or adapt to new requirements.

Now it is your turn:

BPMN EXERCISE 2

Once you've read the Fizzit case examples here, you should begin to understand how BPMN works and in how it can relate to a business perspective as in the business concept model. Why don't you try:

Draw a business process modelling notation diagram for the Fizzit case showing the activities for when the Customer takes the items to the drop-off location to when the items are collected by the Courier.

You can find an answer in the Solutions Appendix 1.

We now move on to problem frames and into the section of the book that has a requirements analysis focus.

Notes

1 Peter Checkland (1981), *Systems Thinking, Systems Practice*, Wiley. Further works have appeared by Checkland and Jim Scholes, all of which are excellent. I list the original here, still available at time of writing on Amazon. Soft Systems Methodology is an approach that has stood the test of time.

2 The official and updated specification for BPMN can be found here: http://www.bpmn.org/

3 Martyn Ould (2005), *Business Process Management*, British Computer Society. Ould created Role Activity Diagrams as a way to model processes from a role-based perspective, arguing correctly from my point of view, that we need to know who is doing what, not just what is being done. It is a shame that RADs did not become more popular in practice because they are the best of all business process modelling approaches I have seen purely from a business perspective. Ould's material is freely available from his consulting business: http://www.veniceconsulting.co.uk/. There are plenty of downloads here, including a Visio stencil – which is a bit fiddly to install – and a full online version of his excellent book.

4 UML Activity Diagrams normally form a chapter in texts on UML (Unified Modelling Language – a set of modelling tools for describing software, especially the design of object-oriented systems). Take your pick, there are a lot of books out there. I still prefer the works by the 'Three Amgos': James Rumbaugh, Ivar Jacobsen and Grady Booch, the original creators of UML. The official specification for UML can be found here: https://www.uml.org/.

Chapter 3

Problem Frames

Michael Jackson – the renowned software engineer and thinker (not the singer) – created the requirements framing approach he called *problem frames*.[1] The idea of the problem frame is to marry context with requirements for a specific type of problem to be solved. The great thing about problem frames is that they are excellent at narrowly scoping development problems to one type of problem. This idea can help in determining the products we must deliver as part of project management. Before we get to this purpose, let us first describe the elements of problem frames. Please note that the notation comes direct from Jackson's work.

Elements of the Problem Frame

There are really three key parts to problem frames. 1. Domains (causal and biddable), 2. Machines and 3. Requirements. The domains represent physical things that are controlled e.g. the lights unit in Figure 3.1. A user of a system is called a biddable domain on the grounds that humans should behave in certain ways but may not do so. The machine domain is the computer we need to programme. The requirements oval contains the requirements for those specific domains that the requirements are connected to. The idea behind problem frames is to identify which requirements match to what domains. The problem frame in Figure 3.1 is called a *required behaviour frame* in that the lights unit is required to behave in accordance to the rules determined by the light regime as set out in the requirements. The Lights Controller is what gets programmed to make this happen. 'a' represents the specification in

DOI: 10.1201/9781003168119-3

41

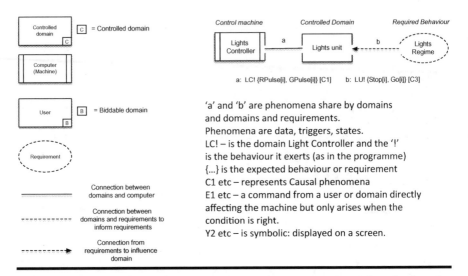

Figure 3.1 Elements of problem frames. 'a' and 'b' are phenomena share by domains and domains and requirements. Phenomena are data, triggers, states. LC! – is the domain Light Controller and the '!' is the behaviour it exerts (as in the programme). {...} is the expected behaviour or requirement. C1 etc – represent Causal phenomena. E1 etc – command from a user or domain directly affecting the machine but only arises when the condition is right. Y2 etc – is symbolic: displayed on a screen.

terms of how the machine and domain must operate. 'b' indicates which requirements impact which domain.

An extension of the required behaviour frame is the *commanded behaviour frame* as depicted in Figure 3.2.

In this example, we have introduced an operator who has the task of determining when the lights units change from red to green and back again. This situation could arise at a significant road works when it is not easy to maintain acceptable flow of traffic through automated timings; it requires on-the-spot decisions and only a human can make such good value judgements.

With the information superhighway going into overdrive, we can find just about anything. Jackson has a frame for this called the *information display frame*. Its focus is more on output than working out the algorithm for finding the information. Figure 3.3 shows an information display frame for a satellite navigation system that you might have in your car.

The current location (real-world domain), unless you are stationary, is moving. The requirement is to be able to track the location of where you are. The Monitor computer is the programme that implements this requirement then displays the results on the Sat Nav display for you to

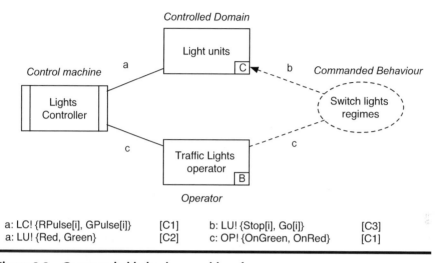

a: LC! {RPulse[i], GPulse[i]}   [C1]   b: LU! {Stop[i], Go[i]}   [C3]
a: LU! {Red, Green}   [C2]   c: OP! {OnGreen, OnRed}   [C1]

Figure 3.2   Commanded behaviour problem frame.

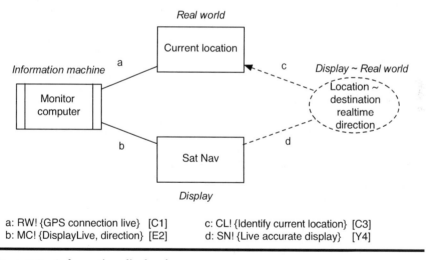

a: RW! {GPS connection live}   [C1]   c: CL! {Identify current location} [C3]
b: MC! {DisplayLive, direction} [E2]   d: SN! {Live accurate display}   [Y4]

Figure 3.3   Information display frame.

see. Of course, there are satellites that locate where you are and your device must contact and remain connected with a set of satellites in order for it to calculate your location. Nonetheless, the key consideration is the display for us.

Most of us engage in productivity software these days. This book you are reading was typed out using Microsoft Word, a text-editor productivity tool. The problem frame for this is a called the *simple workpieces*

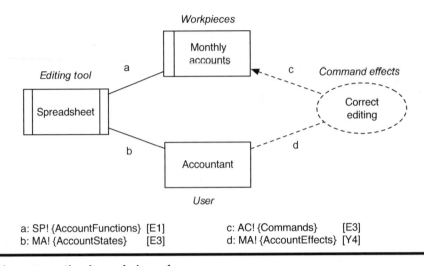

a: SP! {AccountFunctions} [E1]   c: AC! {Commands}   [E3]
b: MA! {AccountStates}   [E3]   d: MA! {AccountEffects} [Y4]

Figure 3.4   Simple workpieces frame.

frame. A workpiece is the electronic document we are working on; a real piece of work!

Figure 3.4 shows that the workpiece, the monthly accounts file (note the different domain design), is open in an editing tool, the Spreadsheet. The accountant user simply follows the correct editing rules or requirements to command the spreadsheet tool to change the monthly accounts file as desired.

The final frame we will consider here (though others have been proposed since Jackson published his works) is called the *transformation frame*. The purpose of this frame is to convert one set of data into another type. Figure 3.5 provides an example.

In the example, the software tool is a 'security analyser' that will run a parse through a set of emails (the input) to try to identify whatever the requirements ask for, the rules of the analysis. The output is a report describing the findings of the parse.

Making Use of Problem Frames When We Can

There is a great deal more to problem frames analysis. There are all the symbols I've managed to avoid writing about (Jackson believes in formalisms) and there is something called a frame concern. This is a description of how the problem frame and requirements work to address the type of system to be built and type of problem to be solved. I won't go into frame concerns here because it is a big and not so straightforward

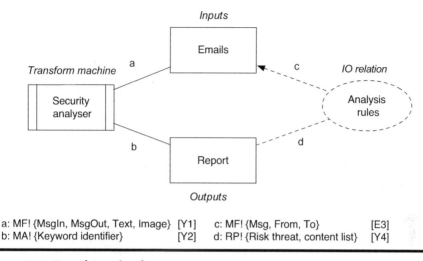

a: MF! {MsgIn, MsgOut, Text, Image} [Y1]   c: MF! {Msg, From, To}   [E3]
b: MA! {Keyword identifier}   [Y2]   d: RP! {Risk threat, content list} [Y4]

Figure 3.5   Transformation frame.

topic. I would ask readers who are interested or curious to read more on this topic direct from Jackson's *Problem Frames*, itself.

For us, problem frames are useful in helping determine what type of system we are building, what types of systems (according to Jackson's classification) we need to know about. Something we need to think about in our situation is how a problem frame informs us of what we need to produce and also returning the other way, how a product breakdown structure – described later in the book – may help us in determining how to frame our problem or structure our proposed solution.

I wrote in the sub-header 'when we can'. What do I mean here? I prefer to think of the early lifecycle work that is addressed here as problem describing and sometimes solving. The thing with problems is that they are different, have different contexts, address different issues. To solve different problems, you need different tools. The tool or tools you use need to be appropriate to solving the problem at hand or at least in identifying it, then describing it as accurately as possible. There may be times when problem frames won't add to your understanding. The same is true for all the requirements and business tools described in this book. We do need a list of requirements in all cases and better they are in a table. For without such a table it is impossible to schedule the project or conduct it successfully.

Now that I have introduced problem frames and then said don't bother unless you have to, I think it is a good idea to show you what is so good about problem frames by presenting some examples. But first, what's good about problem frames?

The brilliance of problem frames is the recognition that requirements analysis is not simply drawing up a list of basic requirements along the lines of: the system should do... You can do this and ultimately there will be a list (see the next chapter!) but problem frames offer something far above this. They give you the ability to design a system as it is meant to work in a modular way. In other words, the system you are going to build may have various core functions, of which some are quite unique to specific areas of the system. Complex systems such as e-commerce sites or ERP systems are composed of several, differing core functions. There are reporting functions, document preparation functions, control functions (automated and human operated), parsing functions and so on. If you have a long list of requirements capturing how the system should do things, it's easy to brush over the importance of separation of concerns. A separation of concern is the ability to separate disparate and non-connecting functions of a system. Let's take a very well-known tool: Google Translate. It's simple to use. You have text written in, say Chinese, and you want to translate it into English. You type in the text (or cut-and-paste) sort of like a text editor, or Workpiece in problem frames parlance. Once the language is typed in and assuming the tool recognises the language you've entered, it will automatically translate it into English (this is the Transformation frame) if English is the chosen output language. If Translate doesn't recognise the language you input, or you want it translated into a different language from English, then you can select the language of choice to do this. So, you have two problem frames, both with highly different functions but both in the same product. Granted, the Workpiece is the most basic form of a document. You simply enter text. You could quite rightly justify only a requirements list here and say, all Translate does is allow text editing so a Workpiece is a bit much really. But what if the translation is incorrect? And between English and Chinese, the literal meaning is often not the same. You have the ability to correct the translation and store this within the translator. So now you can manipulate text that comes out of the transformation and correct it. The manipulating and correcting of text is part of the Workpiece problem frame.

For such a simple visual idea – translating one language into another – it is more complicated still yet something we may take for granted. If we view the left input box as a Workpiece, no matter how simple it is, the right side of the display presents the translated text. This makes it is an Information Display frame.

In a way, problem frames don't make the life of the analyst less complex – there's extra work, and thinking about the problem, drawing out the diagram and so on. The analyst doesn't necessarily learn much more about the problem. But problem frames are a powerful tool for making the life of the developer a lot less complex and it is the analyst's job to make this happen.

Multiframe Problem for Google Translate

Figure 3.6 shows what is called a *multiframe* problem frame for Google Translate. It's a combination of different problem frames that combine to form the requirements and domains of interest for the system in one figure. It would also be fine to describe separate problem frames but in the end, we need to build one system, not three. The multiframe is formed of the Basic Workpiece, Translation and Information Display

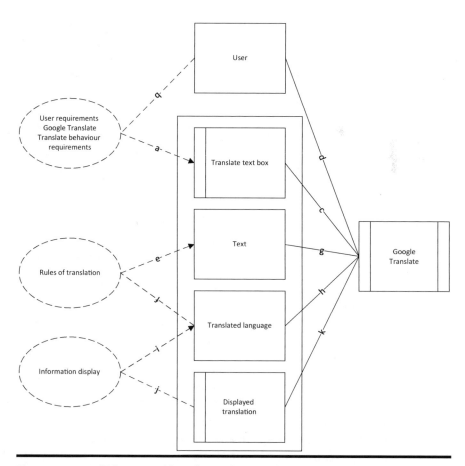

Figure 3.6 Multiframe problem frame for Google Translate.

frames. This is the thing with problem frames – they can make life a little bit harder when the obvious may be good enough. For instance, it may well be good enough to keep the problem frames separate (see above for examples) than combined. It may well be good enough to not bother at all. As I will continue to write and have written already: pick and use the tools that match the problem. What's key to remember with problem frames is that this is what they actually help you to do: pick the right tools to analyse and build the solution for specific problem types. Problem frames are really patterns.

Even though I am writing this book and should really know what I am talking about, I do have to admit it took a bit of a leap to include the Information Display frame. The Workpiece actually manages a display otherwise the user could not type or paste in the text to be translated. But the Workpiece presumes the display and the workpiece (document) is one and the same. I have chosen to include the information display here because this is an output screen, separate from the workpiece. I get the feeling from Jackson's work that he had in mind something like the example above: a GPS or representation of something in the real world in a different way rather than simply displaying text. Nonetheless, the user cannot do much other than copy the text in the display. If the translation isn't as correct as it could be then the user won't work on changing the text in the display but elsewhere. As such, the Workpiece is elsewhere or could even be a simple rule change in the transformation frame requirements set. For example, a word may be incorrectly translated in a specific sentence and the user may select to update the translation record within Google Translate. That then becomes something different to only Information Display or only Workpiece but much more a combination of these two coupled with the Transformation frame.

We've identified the domains of interest and a set of requirements for Google Translate. We have not yet defined the requirements or specification (a–k) in the example above but include a first pass at this in Table 3.1. Eventually, we would have to be a lot more precise about each of the requirement and specification phenomena. For now, it's just about good enough to know the most basic of relationship. I used the term phenomena above because this is the language of Jackson. What it means is something physical or otherwise that guides, moves, controls or affects the system behaviour. Requirements phenomena are biddable with regard to the user. In other words, the user can only do certain things on the Workpiece according to how Google Translator works. It's called biddable because the user doesn't have to do as the requirements state. A user could drop an image into the text box but it would not be

Table 3.1   Problem Frames Requirements Table

Problem Frame	Label	Description
Workpiece	a	Text typed, allow text changes
	b	Input text for translation; select language to translate to
	c	Recognise text; reject input
	d	Display text
Transformation	e	Identified text (language, phrases, words, characters)
	f	Translated output matches input
	g	Capture text
	h	Translate output for display
Information Display	i	Capture text in correct format
	j	Display translation
	k	Formatting and display parameters

translated. However, the 'translated' text box on the right has to behave according to the requirement of providing a translation of the text input by the user. If the user attempts to put anything other than text into the text box (included here are all the world's languages), then the system would be required to not translate it, to display an instruction message such as 'insert text only' or do nothing at all, dependent upon the requirement. It cannot deviate from this.

The multiframe problem frame (Figure 3.6) combines machine domains into one but not the requirements sets. This is an important distinction because though we are building one system, we need to ensure it behaves exactly as we wish, so a separation of concerns regarding functionality is vital. We must focus on the right requirements in the right context. The difficult part will be the points where the frames connect to work seamlessly as a complete system. However hard this may be, it will be much easier because we have designed the system to work as in its independent parts as separated as possible. The design domains – Translate text box, Text, Translated Language, Displayed Translation (the striped boxes are 'screens') – are all found at the interface of the Translate machine. This is why they are boxed together. We cannot design a user even if we wanted to. There has been discussion in the problem frames community about users whose job is scripted, such as call centre operators and cold callers. They follow a designed path to respond to your answers to their questions. This scripting may or may not be automated within the system and as such we simply consider the script as the requirements governing a Workpiece where answers are input and the next prompt emerges, such as in a survey. Or it could be a commanded behaviour domain where the behaviour of a physical object is determined by the choices made by a user, such as when you might be within a virtual reality world. There has been a problem frame proposed for this concept[2] and given today's very high-tech gaming world, it might have some traction.

One thing to mention before I forget: the notation for problem frames from the example frames at the start of the chapter, in reference to phenomena, that is requirements and specification, is a little odd. Basically, if it says BA! {...}, the exclamation mark ! means the domain BA is responsible for the requirement or specification within the squiggly brackets. The square brackets afterwards with C, E and Y inside the brackets represents the kind of phenomena to expect. C is causal – because I press this button it causes something to always happen. E is a command event – in the event of x occurring do something. Y represents what is displayed on a screen. If you remember, a key/explanation is found at the start of this chapter. This has always been an overly complex part of the problem frames approach and I don't particularly think it helpful or straightforward. You will see, looking back, that I ignore it in the examples. Nor do I mention it in the requirements Table 3.1. Whether you choose to use this is up to you. If I were writing this for an academic conference, I would use it. But in practice, I am not so sure.

Problem frames as an approach to systems analysis has a great deal more to it than the very brief outline provided for you here. There is something called a frame concern, for instance. This is a walkthrough 'proof' to test the validity of any specific frame in meeting the requirement or problem description. It's a bit beyond where we are now. If you want to learn more on this, I recommend you read Jackson's tome *Problem Frames*. There are other even more brilliant ideas in the book such as the progression of problems. I will address this later in the chapter but only in a perfunctory way. Others have used the concept of a progression of problems to help solve massive business problems, such as strategic alignment.[3] I will come back to the progression of problems notion in a minute but first I think it a good idea you try to model a couple of problem frames.

PROBLEM FRAMES EXERCISE 1

Now that you've seen the multiframe for Google Translate, let's take a step back. Below are two tasks, one hopefully straightforward, and one that may need a bit more thinking about.

1. Draw the Basic Workpieces problem frame.

2. Now that the simple answer is done in question 1, let's try something more complicated. *Imagine that Google Translate has a new function. Translated text has a physical control capability. In other words, if you inputted 'open door' in English, the translation in Chinese would actually open the door. A real door. It's a silly idea. But imagine you're on holiday in Beijing and your hotel is state-of-the-tech. If you speak Chinese, you can command your room to behave as you say: lights on, lights off, close door, open door and so on. But if you are a non-Chinese speaker, you can now use Google Translate, which has a voice function, to speak for you.* Draw the Commanded Behaviour problem frame for this.

The solutions can be found in Solutions Appendix 1.

Progression of Problems

I wanted to briefly talk more business and to look at strategic matters. Jackson presented an interesting concept called the progression of problems. It appears on only one page of his 300+ page book *Problem Frames* but it is something quite profound. The idea underlying such a progression is that IT solutions often begin conceptually as a business problem or opportunity to be addressed. Those opportunities are captured in strategy language and expressed perhaps as business strategy or objectives. A command then filters down to the technical and operational people to build a system to make it work. Those technical people do their best to interpret the command, filtered by layers of management in between. But there's a translation confusion – the original, brilliant idea has been inadvertently altered, misunderstood or even manipulated so that the end result is not what the executive wanted. This occurs regularly and is called strategic misalignment. The goal, therefore, is to devise a traceable way to show how a solution does meet the strategy and that the requirement does not get altered on its journey from the executive down to the shop floor and back up again. Jackson may not have been thinking exactly about this, but having had pizza with him one evening before a conference on problem frames I chaired, I suspect he had been. Certainly, he would have experienced such frustrating communication breakdowns in his work many times. I also suspect with the progression of problems, which is a little bit outside the interest of the rest of the excellent *Problem Frames* book, Jackson was throwing it out there for others to pick up. Anyway, let's take a look at the concept.

Let's begin by ignoring the curved corner boxes such as that around all the Computer (Machine) domains in Figure 3.7. We'll come back to this in a moment. But let's read the diagram horizontally. The bottom layer has a requirements set RE directly connected to the Computer. This set, RE, is the specification or the behavioural rules that drive the computer. The next level up, requirements RD, has a domain DD between it and the Computer. What this means is the requirements need to have some impact outside of the computer in domain DD. The next level has two domains, DD and DC. Both of these have to feel the impact of the requirements set RC, as implemented in the Computer. And so on to the top level, RA, where there are four domains between the Computer and the requirements. The further away from the computer, the closer to the business needs you get.

Strategically, we can also consider that at the RA requirements level, we are in the realm of business strategy, if we were to model problems with this in mind. Then RB might be tactics and objectives to achieve the highest-level goals in the strategic view of RA. Moving down, we can see RC and this could be business process requirements to support achievement of the tactics (which support strategies) and objectives (that support the goals of RA).[4] When we enter the RD level, where we are one domain removed from the Computer, we are in problem frames territory and we can begin to specify the requirements. RE is all about the solution itself.

Let's look from a different perspective now. Figure 3.8 shows labels with regard to influence or where in the world we need to consider domains. Imagine we are modelling an e-commerce business. We have several 'roles' involved in the business. We have, reading left to right, an IT Department, Accounts Department, Inventory. Then we have the e-commerce site itself, and finally a Customer who will make purchases on the site. These purchases are fulfilled by Inventory (or stores) having stock for fulfil the order, an Accounts Department to process payments and an IT Department making sure all connecting systems from the Customer's e-commerce site, the Inventory control system, the Accounting system and Customer Records cooperate.

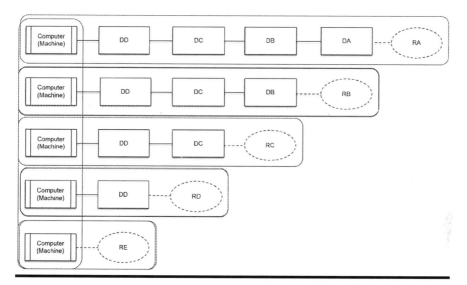

Figure 3.7   Progression of problems (adapted from Jackson's *Problem Frames*).

RA contains the requirements for how a Customer is expected to use the site. So, if you were ordering a book from an online bookseller you would need to document how a Customer would use the system. The curved-edged box outlining RA and domain DA delineate that we should be concerned with the Customer and how the e-commerce site is used from the Customer perspective.

RB would contain requirements specific to the e-commerce site itself such as user experience design requirements, what buttons are where, how they are expected to behave and how aspects of the system may need to interface with other systems. The curved-edged box outlining RB and domain DB delineate that we should be concerned with the e-commerce site primarily. But we also include domain DA to ensure we have addressed how the e-commerce site is used from the Customer perspective. The two DB domains are in fact one and the same domain. Figure 3.7 shows the grouping of domains and requirements horizontally meaning there is only one DB and it only becomes of interest when we are at the requirements levels RB and RA.

RC would contain requirements specific to the inventory, domain DC, and the inventory system, in how it connects to the e-commerce site (domain DB) and how it behaves with regards to automated stock updates and orders. There may be a track-and-trace system (e.g. RFID) in place within the warehouse for specific stock items that have been ordered. We might consider whether the Customer has visibility to this or not. Also, we need to include any specific interface requirements or

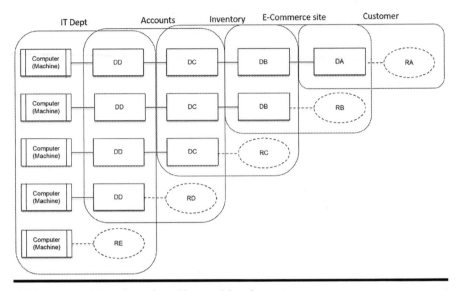

Figure 3.8 Progression of problems with role names.

even APIs for connecting with the Accounts system. We may also want to think about stock ordering by providing interfaces to Procurement/Purchasing as part of a wider supply chain management.

RD are Accounts requirements. We must address the Accounts domain of interest, DD. This can be financial and order fulfilment, dealing with payments and customer records. We need to consider systems interfaces also. Accounts has to ensure Customer payments occur appropriately so will deal with external organisations like banks by providing electronic account access.

RE is the specification of the Computer (Machine) within the IT Department or IT service company managing the various systems within the Value Chain (RE to RA).

I don't want to go further into the progression of problems here. It is ably described in the various academic papers with regards to strategy.[5] Suffice to say, I don't think Jackson explored it to the depth he may have wished. It is certainly the case that he was on to a very useful idea but I think it was slightly beyond the scope of his book. What is beyond the scope of this book you now are reading is further discussion of problem frames as a standalone technique. There is a great deal more that could be discussed and I point you to Jackson's works since they are the best and they are the original. There are actually two things to consider before we wrap up the chapter though and they relate to two specific questions: what happens next and what happened last?

Deriving Problem Frames from Business Processes

Before we get to the next chapter we must go back a step and work out how we can derive problem frames from BPMN models. The relationship between the two models is relatively clear for some aspects. Table 3.2 lists the elements that are part of the Business Process Modelling Notation (BPMN) that have a corresponding element in problem frames.

Table 3.2 BPMN and Problem Frame Links

BPMN Element	Problem Frame Element	Explanation
Pool	Domain of interest, Machine (possibly)	Fizzit's BPMN would have pools such as Customer, TWOO, Fizzit. Each could be a domain of interest. We might have to consider also the Machine domain if we are explicit about Fizzit's website in BPMN.
Swimlane	Domain of interest, Machine (possibly)	Swimlanes such as Customer Accounts, Courier, Warehouse within Fizzit's pool in BPMN. Each could be a domain of interest. We might have to consider also the Machine domain if we are explicit about e.g. Fizzit's website in BPMN.
Message	Shared phenomena	A message from one pool to another in BPMN might contain data or an email or document or even a command that could be considered as phenomena between two domains of interest or a domain and the machine.
Thread of control between swimlanes	Connection between domains and shared phenomena	A thread passes control of a process from one swimlane to another and within a swimlane. That thread isn't just a command but can also include data.
Actions within tasks, timers, decision gateways	Requirements, specification	Elements of BPMN that are doing things can be functional requirements and constraints on behaviour of the system (which are part of requirements specification).

One last thing to think about is that the actions described as tasks in a business process can indicate what type of (sub)system we might consider in terms of a problem frame. I write '(sub)' in relation to system because as you have seen, most systems have enough different elements in them to have multiple problem frames. We can call these different problem frames, subsystems.

Now that we have a problem frame we can start to think about some key aspects of moving forwards: what products (designs, documents, etc.) we need to build a system, and also about the structure or architecture of the system. That's found later once we commence with the project management aspect of this book. But first let us move on to 'conventional' requirements and specification documentation.

Notes

1 Michael Jackson (2000), *Problem Frames*, ACM Press. This was Jackson's complete work on problem frames but his original thoughts were published in his iconic lexicon: *Software Requirements and Specifications* (1995) ACM Press as well as in several academic papers.

2 Ian Bray and Karl Cox (2003), *The Simulator: Another Elementary Problem Frame?* Proceedings of REFSQ'03, Springer-Verlag.

3 S. Bleistein, K. Cox, J. Verner and K. Phalp (2006), *Requirements Engineering for e-Business Advantage*, Requirements Engineering Journal, 11 (1), pp. 4–16. We wrote a lot more papers addressing this subject but this is a reasonable place to start.

4 The idea of objectives supporting more abstract goals and tactics supporting broader strategies comes from the Business Rules Group, who in the 1990s and 2000s were pushing their concept called The Business Motivational Model – how elements of strategic requirements (strategy, vision, mission, goals, etc.) supported each other coherently. Their lead name contributor was John Zachman of the Zachman Framework fame. Their concepts really resonated with me and I think they still make a lot of sense. Many of these people were involved in business rules and business concepts, as described in Chapter 1. More on the BRG can be found here: http://www.businessrules-group.org/theBRG.htm

5 Progression of problems was deployed to help model the concept of strategic alignment. Here is a useful reference: S. Bleistein, K. Cox and J. Verner (2006), *Validating Strategic Alignment of Organisational IT Requirements using Goal Modeling and Problem Diagrams*, Journal of Systems and Software, 79 (3), pp. 362–378. The paper details how the combination of models was put together in the context of the progression of problems to address the big issue of helping solve strategic alignment.

Chapter 4

Requirements and Specification

A requirement can be defined as something someone wants or needs. This means that all of what we've discussed so far in this book could qualify as requirements. Business rules are requirements for how the business works. A business concept diagram shows a perspective on how those requirements of business relate to the context of business. Business process models show how systems for making or producing things can be described. As-is processes – describing how the business functions now – can be defined as process requirements. To-be processes, the same. Problem frames explicitly document requirements and specification phenomena that allow you to determine the type of system to be built. If any need could be a requirement, could we not think it unnecessary to document requirements separate from all of the above approaches? Yes, we could think it unnecessary but we will need to document some things about requirements.

Specification is the detailing of the requirement from the perspective of inputs and outputs, data models and constraints. We might even use formalisms (such as predicate logic) in order to write a 'better' requirements document. It must be stated here that this chapter does not address all the ways in which requirements and specifications can be written or modelled – this not the point. Previous chapters have addressed modelling and the following one, on use cases, continues this. There are many ways to model requirements and other approaches you may find are more suitable to the situation you are in.

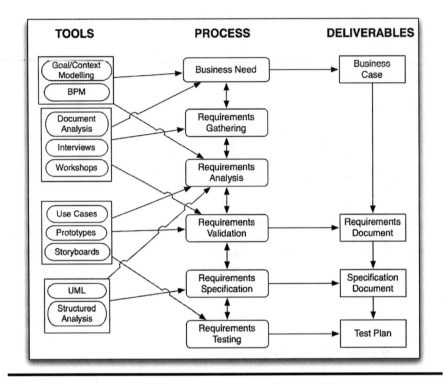

Figure 4.1 Basic requirements process, tools and deliverables.

An overview of a requirements process, with tools used and documents produced is found in Figure 4.1. This isn't the be-all, end-all especially with regard to the tools. What you see is my experience; that is, tools I have used and where they fit in the early software development lifecycle.

Figure 4.1 is three columns interconnected. The left column lists tools, such as BPM (business process modelling), use cases and so on. These tools are valuable at different or overlapping phases of the requirements process:

1. Business need or opportunity identified (that requires software support) and can be modelled for instance as a business concept model or a goal-context model or business process model or all of these, and more. These are documented in a business case. They can also be part of a business analysis document or a business process document.
2. Requirements are gathered (for the software or process, for instance) using tools such as interviews, document analysis or

workshops – none of which are addressed in detail in this book. There are plenty of good sources on elicitation of requirements.

3. The requirements are analysed to make sure they make sense and various tools such as BPMN or use cases, for instance, are used to help in this – only if needed though. I keep making this point and will continue to do so: use the tools only when you need to. Don't waste time designing UML sequence diagrams if they offer very little to developers on a particular project. Don't run interviews if time is short and a workshop is more practical. Conversely, if you have interviewed all stakeholders, you probably don't need a workshop. So please pick and choose the right time to use the right tool. What you do use is entirely context dependent.

4. A requirements validation occurs with the customer and user(s), and an output of validation is a requirements document. Prototypes and/or storyboards can assist in this. Problem frames could work here too.

5. Those requirements needing further examination are specified and this is documented in a specification. Tools to assist in clarifying requirements can be UML or other modelling tools.

6. Requirements can also be used as the basis for software testing so it is feasible to begin creation of the test documentation, either as scenarios or another format.

7. Note that the tools introduced to you in this book cover the end-to-end early lifecycle. They are sufficient to address most situations in your degree. You could swap scenario analysis for use cases – and I actually prefer scenarios. But use cases are very popular so they win out. You could add persona analysis to understand more about users. If you need to do so, then do so. That's perfectly fine and of benefit to you.

One last comment on Figure 4.1: The process appears top-down though in practice it is often middle out or bottom up. Whichever way it is, the key is to ensure that you cover what you need, not more than you need, in sufficient detail for *you* to really know what your client needs and to give developers a good understanding of what is needed to programme the system.

More about Requirements

As we have said, a general definition of a requirement could be: *A requirement is something wanted or needed*. The weakness to this all-encompassing definition is that it is all-encompassing. We need a little more precision so I recommend the following definition:

> Requirements are all of the capabilities and constraints a (software) product must meet in the real world that helps address the customer's opportunity.

Let's stick with the more specific definition because of the pretext for this book ostensibly on the topic of requirements (in the guise of business and technology perspectives) for software systems or applications. I did not use the 'problem' word in the definition because software can present opportunities as well as help solve identifiable problems. A software system may open up possibilities not foreseen: a solution looking for an opportunity, not a solution looking for a problem, though there are plenty of these in the tech world. As such, I use 'opportunity' in the above definition in case we want to be more optimistic about the world, which we ought to try to be.

Types of Requirements

We've looked at business definitions, process definitions, and the concept of capturing a potential IT solution in or as a 'frame'. All of these we can call requirements but not all of these will fit our requirements definition as we move from a business view to a technical, software view, which is what we must do if we are to build solutions for the opportunities identified in business. We can generalise four basic types of requirements.

Business Requirements: Describe what results the business wants to achieve after the new system has been built. We have discussed business rules in Chapter 1 so rather than use the label business requirement, it is better that we are consistent with terminology and will stick to business rule. Chapter 1 explains what a business rule is and I do not wish to repeat myself here. I will say that business strategy – which can also be labelled as a business requirement – is different to a business rule. I look at a rule as an explicit description of how an aspect of a business must function to achieve the goal of a part of that business, be it a business function or process. Strategy sits above this and provides abstract ways in which a business ought to operate. Strategies are broken into tasks (following the Business Rules Group definition) and these tasks clearly achieve objectives, which are measurable and comparable to say, a key performance indicator definition and metric.

User Requirements: Describe what a user needs the system to do to achieve the business requirements. There is a great deal of work in academia and practice on user requirements. Agile methods prefer to talk in user stories. Software engineering traditionally (since UML at least) speaks in use cases. Human–computer interaction describes scenarios of system usage. With no apology I can say, having experienced all of them (user stories, use cases, scenarios) that they are all of a muchness. There are nuances and the key differences tend to emerge with what you write the user story or scenario on – an index card or post-it note versus the use case description, which is longer so needs an A4 sheet of paper. Use cases tend to be more system-centric. I really love scenarios. They have been around for a long time and they are a mature tool. I also like user stories and I like index cards because they are flexible. Better than post-it notes. However, I am going to focus on use cases in this book because it is the standard way to document user-system interaction. I don't think it is the best but it is the standard. User stories may well be leading the charge now, especially if your project is agile, but user stories don't cover the detailed ground you will need that use cases do.

Functional Requirements: Describe activities or processes that the software must perform to achieve the user requirements and business rules. The entire focus of the functional requirement is the function of the system at its interfaces. Use cases are good for this.

Non-functional or Quality Requirements: Describe performance and capability objectives the system must achieve. Also, security and privacy requirements fit into this classification, sort of. They are out of scope of this book for now but may appear in a later volume.

Business requirements are covered in Chapters 1 and 2 but we will touch on them here again. User requirements describe what someone does when in need of interacting with software. We've looked at user requirements indirectly with the BPMN user task type and with biddable user domains in problem frames. We'll be a lot more specific on this with use cases in the next chapter. Functional requirements are explained by use cases in that we are explicitly concerned with the functioning of the system. We will look at what I call 'specification' later, which is explicit to addressing functions. Non-functional requirements are those that are not focussed on the user interacting with the system but with the function of the system working properly itself. Confusing? Totally. When I first encountered non-functional requirements in the 1990s, I have to admit I made a joke about them: these are the requirements that don't work! I've stuck with the joke and have not gotten over the silly choice of name for them. Thankfully, a few other names have appeared: performance requirements (SCRU → speed, capacity, reliability, usability[1]) but these are a subset of a bigger generalisation, quality requirements. I like this term because something of quality implies it has, well… quality, which is good. So, let's drop the 'non-functional' negative and focus on quality.

In terms of documenting requirements, I prefer tables to any models we may have. But before we get to the tables, let's look a bit more closely at the differences in requirements:

Example Business Requirement

BR1. Increase call centre productivity in managing customer requests by 25 per cent or more over the next financial year.

The first thing to note is that we have used the term 'business requirement.' So! We simply cannot pigeonhole everything as a business rule. We are dealing with a statement pertaining to a business objective. It's almost a key performance indicator. There's no mention of technology. There is an efficiency percentage included. The word 'productivity' is prominent. We are discussing a department labelled 'call centre'. We are talking finances. Clearly, this is not going to be a software requirement. It's business.

Example User Requirement

UR7. The call centre operator needs to verify the particulars of each caller to establish if the caller is a new or existing customer.

This is a user requirement on the grounds we are referring to the subject of the requirements as a call centre operator. The system to be built will be used by the call centre operator. Note that the customer is also referred to here and that there is still no mention of a technical solution. We might be tempted to call this a business rule, as it were. But I prefer to think of this as a process or workflow step done by a human and so can label it a user requirement.

Example Functional Requirement

FR3. Call centre operator inputs customer reference number into system and system retrieves customer name, address and account information.

We might be tempted to call this requirement a user requirement. I can see why. The requirement describes a user, the call centre operator, using the system. But the requirement goes further than this and describes what the system must do in response. We are being explicit here: the system is in scope and must respond to a user input.

Example Quality Requirement

QR3.1. System performs FR3 retrieval in less than 30 seconds 95 per cent of the time with ≤ 200 call centre operators logged in at the same time.

The quality requirement puts a time constraint on the successful function of the system. Provided the system can manage this time frame appropriately, we need not concern ourselves with graceful – or otherwise – degradation. This is also a capacity requirement and please note the reference back to functional requirement 3 (FR3) above. Whenever you have a function, you can also have a quality associated to that function, and vice versa. It's not always necessary to associate a quality requirement with a functional requirement but if you have a specific condition to be met, then do so. This means when we put together a requirements document, we don't always need to consider the quality requirement. The function will always operate within the actual quality parameters of the system irrespective. But there are times we need to make it clear what those parameters are. In this example, it's important that the business function with this number of call centre operators working as normally as possible. Once we go over this threshold of 200 staff, then perhaps the system really might become slower. You may have experienced this when calling a utility to pay a bill, for example. The employee might say, 'sorry the computer is slow today.' This might be because it is exceeding its stated capacity requirement.

REQUIREMENTS TYPE IDENTIFICATION EXERCISE 1

Name which kind of requirement (business, user, functional, quality) the following statements are:

1. Deliver 15% performance improvement in output of products off production line.
2. User must provide two forms of identification before new account opening process begins.
3. The light must change from red to green when 'Go' button is pressed.
4. The change from red to green must occur within 0.5 seconds and remain green for a further 120 seconds.
5. New product features result in capturing 10% more market share.
6. The system displays the customer booking prior to credit card payment as confirmation.
7. If the user drops the phone on a hard surface from less than 2 meters, there should be no degradation of function or effect on the performance of the phone.

Answers can be found in the Solutions Appendix 1.

Ways to Gather Requirements

Although I said I won't address requirements elicitation in detail, I will make some comments on some of the techniques more commonly used.

Interviews –I have addressed interviews in great detail my book, *Strategic Requirements Analysis*. As such, I will not comment further here.

Workshops[2] – if you have the opportunity to get 10-15 people into a room all at the same time for a day (or even half a day) then do it rather than interviewing. You will have to have a colleague available as a scribe who can keep statements up-to-date live on a screen projected in the room. You let the participants discuss their jobs and how they work together in processes and with records, for instance. You document the key things they need in their job (a first pass at requirements). Once you believe you've got everything you can from these people, who should come from varied roles in the organisation or are touched by the system in some way, send them home! Go through the document to identify inconsistencies and then send these out to participants for clarification. Once done, put the whole document together and work to get it validated and signed off. This is a long process but instead of spending a week interviewing, you can get everything elicited in a day. A day or two of analysis and you're ready to get some feedback. A downside is the risk that staff are not willing to talk openly in front of senior members of staff. I ran a brainstorming session once to elicit the needs of a media department for a new inventory system. No one talked except to say yes and no. Why was this? Their boss was there and no one liked her!

Experience the user life – it used to be suggested you could experience life as a user by taking their place on certain tasks. I think this is a bit risky because that user has potentially spent years in that role. What are you going to learn in one hour or even one day? The general outcome of this can only be a dumbing down of any issues because you just have not been there long enough to experience them. You also run the risk of insulting the user – who would complain – by implying that when you did the job there were no problems or the user's solutions just did not seem to make sense. Avoid. I've tried it and found exactly what I wrote above!

Observation – is known technically as ethnography and is the long-term study of a situation such as office life. I like this approach but it is really only a research tool for longitudinal studies. In practice, you cannot really afford to spend more than a few hours observing people at work. You'll find they behave differently because you're a novelty and they know they are being observed. It can take time for people to forget you exist. Do if you have time and really get on well with the people you are observing. I did this once on a project because I did have time and I did get on well with the people I was observing. The results were excellent.

Client/user role play – you could ask employees to act out their job and speak aloud what they are doing/thinking. I tried this once and it did not work. I ran the following elicitation tasks: interviews, workshop, brainstorming, role play and observation with one group of stakeholders, all in relation to the new system needed. I found that nothing much aligned. What people actually did, differed from their role play and from interviewing, workshopping or brainstorming sessions. It was only when I created scenarios and a prototype of the system that I began to find out what was really needed! But that was a rather unique project with rather unique people with a very unique work culture. Not all projects are the same.

Document analysis – you should spend a little time reviewing existing documentation on a system, if it is available. It may not make any sense but it could be of value. You need to also look at process documents and corporate plans such as strategic planning documents. It is time-consuming but it can assist you. There is a danger, as I found out on one very document-centric project that whichever document I was reading and asking about, it was always out of date! If you notice this trend happening on a project, abandon this approach and go straight to talking.

Examining software – you may wish to play with the existing software. This is a useful thing because most projects are updates or extensions to existing software. Just be wary that what you propose is really addressing a business need that is current and not just fixing a less than perfect function that ultimately doesn't add a lot of value in the current situation.

Now you've gathered loads of information, what do you do? You need to put it all together in a spreadsheet or other similar document. There are ways to determine what is relevant and what is not, such a rough and ready content analysis.[3]

What if there are contradictions in the document you've put together? For example,

- Observation showed that interview feedback is wrong...
- Many users wanted the same requirements as existing system functions but business managers demand a new set of features to match the new business requirements...
- Customers don't want any new features but manufacturers need to sell more phones...
- The marketing department questionnaire suggests what the business and its customers want are poles apart...

What you can do quite rapidly is:

Re-examine business goals, business rules and the budget for the project – what is really vital and what of that is affordable? You could eliminate many of the lower priority business requirements and cut loose those software requirements addressing them. Did you get the right requirements at all? Do any align with the stated goals of the project and are they financially viable? Did your business concept model provide a better understanding of the business need? Are business processes changed because of the new goals? Is where IT is used on business processes now changed?

Eliminate requirements not aligned or viewed as too costly by management or project sponsor. You can't cut requirements without senior management approval. Though I have mentioned cost, it is not easy to judge how much any function is likely to cost. I think the bigger the requirement, the more likely you are to be able to make a judgement call with senior management or the project manager. In the end, the project manager will need to get the agreement of senior management, not to mention customers. Why is it easier to judge cost the more key or large the requirement? My experience is that it is easier to assign a thumb-in-the-air percentage. If a core functional requirement of an online shopping system is credit/debit card payment, you can take a guess that this might be about 10 per cent of the effort needed hence 10 per cent of the cost. It's a wild guess but borne out of experience. If you are examining the minutiae of detail that we will look at with use cases, then it is almost impossible to accurately guess how much a step in a use case will cost. There are use case points estimation techniques but we would not consider performing these calculations normally. It's just too much effort. This does not mean that the use case point effort estimate is any less accurate than our expert judgement. Agile is all about expert judgement because it sees traditional estimation as hopelessly inaccurate and this assertion is backed up by the data.

Ensure priority stakeholders are given necessary 'air time' – you must give weight to stakeholders who are high ranking, such as a Chief Information Officer (CIO), someone in charge of the IT for a company. Or a key end user who has to experience the system every single day. You might view these people as having a much better grasp of the requirements than those who are mostly not using the system but do get some reports from it or use its data. These people are not unimportant and you need to get their requirements. But when push comes to shove, it is the key stakeholders who ought to get their way. If you are forever compromising and simply including everyone's requirements, the result is going to be a big mess. I once had the task, with my team, of reviewing an internal requirements document for a project keeping track of PhD students over different sites of a company I was employed at. This data was important for our key funder, the Australian Government. A contract hire business analyst originally conducted the requirements phase of the project and had produced a document that our CIO viewed with suspicion: too many requirements, too many contradictions and no doubt too costly. So, he asked my team to review the document and effectively revisit the interviews. We did. We cut out 30 per cent of the requirements. We found the key stakeholder in our company for this project – the person reporting directly to government ministers – did not even know this project had been proposed! Yet he was the one who needed the data. No one else did except perhaps the Chief Executive and only if put on the spot. The key stakeholder's requirements were quite different to those originally gathered. We found process models included for processes that did not exist nor were going to exist. We even found a database in the document that did not exist nor was is it ever going to! These had been documented as 'As-Is'. Whoever had told the business analyst these processes and database were real was very wrong. When we asked the business analyst what he did, he said he just wrote down everything everyone said. He said it wasn't his job to do any analysis – to look for inconsistencies, to find alternatives, to organise and structure the requirements appropriately! He also didn't ask interviewees, 'is there anyone else I should be talking to?' We did. That's how we found the key stakeholder. Unfortunately, the contract business analyst was fired.

Approach stakeholders with unresolved contradictions – this usually solves the contradictions. Often it is the way departments name the same things differently that causes confusion. Also, different departments needing the 'same' data often need it in a different way or need a variation of that data item. You need to find out which way it is needed. If you can't resolve conflicts and it is important to do so, go up a level of management and ask for it be resolved from on high.

Go to the project sponsor for final approval to resolve conflicts – this is similar to the last point. The project sponsor is someone who is backing this project from a senior position in the company. You should keep the sponsor in the loop and if there are major conflicts only, go ask their viewpoint. Don't waste their time on tiny issues; you should be able to deal with these little problems yourself.

Make requirements 'public' among stakeholders to get feedback – you can send key stakeholders (and only key stakeholders) the requirements to get them to spot problems and clarify them. You would even highlight the conflicting requirements and ask for a resolution. Don't send the requirements to everyone because much might be confidential. Your project manager or sponsor needs to guide you on this if you are uncertain of the correct procedure.

Much of the above won't be applicable to a student project but as you now know, you will be able to address these situations effectively in your careers should such situations arise.

Specification of Requirements

The idea behind *formal* specification comes down to a belief that all problems and solutions can be modelled mathematically. Though this is theoretically possible for a number of problems and solutions, the huge effort to do so would kill most projects. This is evidenced by the fact that proponents of formal methods can give you a list of all the big systems that were specified formally with a mathematical language. The *countless* other successful systems that exist are evidence that formal methods are not a practical approach to designing systems unless it is absolutely necessary, you have a massive budget and an exceptionally long lead time. However, use of formalisms here and there – where absolutely necessary – can be beneficial because natural language is open to interpretation. You might want to use B or Z or predicate logic on some aspects of development. The key point to remember with formal methods is that they can only be an internal validation of a natural language requirement or specified requirement. So if the requirement or its specification is wrong, then even if the formal representation in a mathematical notation is technically correct, it is still wrong! It is correct in describing the incorrect requirement correctly. In other words, your formalisation of the requirement does not help at all if the requirement is wrong in the first place.

Heavyweight use of models was then considered the next best thing to formal methods. It should be possible to correctly model a system using the models we have looked at (problem frames as a more modern approach, for instance). It should be possible to precisely specify an entire system using UML or statecharts (now part of UML but previously known as state models or state transition diagrams). It should be possible to model control with petri nets or notations deploying that sort of petri net approach. Enactable business process models (those that can semi-automated to step through as a simulation) are petri net-based. We had a world of formal standards for software requirements specification, such as the IEEE Standard 830 published in 1998. Even when this document was followed, projects still failed. Textbooks reflected the standard and the role of the systems analyst was very much focussed in analysing how the software would work by modelling that boundary between systems and users, but mostly internal design of systems.

Since the rise of Agile, specification has taken a nose dive and the IEEE Standard 830-1998 became superseded. Agile standards for documentation are quite different. The idea of producing a complete specification of a system before moving on to coding was viewed as one of the reasons why customers were not happy (because it might be months or even years before customers got to see any software) and why projects failed more (because too much time was spent on analysis, leading to analysis paralysis, the project dying a slow death by a thousand systems analytical cuts). I will point out here that focussing on business models, as in Chapters 1 and 2 of this book was something very much out of scope of a systems analyst, who was interested only with the immediately user-system interaction and then modelling the design of the software functions.

The rise of Agile development led to a lot of IT departments in companies believing that by simply cutting code – eliminating all the analytical and documentary work – they were being agile. They weren't; this was simply hacking and many struggled as a consequence. Over the last decade, it has been found that Agile cannot work all by its barebones self on bigger projects. A higher degree of preparedness was and is needed. Some of that 'old' analysis and specification work is still needed. As such, I am going to walk you through ten steps into how you document and specify a requirement to the point that programmers can get a good idea of how to code it. I won't be using any formal or mathematical modelling, so don't panic, those who are not keen on math.

How to 'Specify' a Requirement in 10 Easy Steps

Here's the list. I will go through each step individually. Note there will be more things to consider once we've done this bit of the work!

1. Take a user or functional requirement
2. Identify if it has any data attached
3. Document the data
4. Is there a process?
5. Document the process
6. Figure out if there are any outputs needed to meet the requirement
7. Figure out the inputs to generate the correct outputs
8. Uniquely identify the specified requirement
9. What is the quality required?
10. What priority is the requirement?

Let's work through an example. Step 1 identifies a requirement:

> The telesales operator needs to verify the customer's current status with the company (in other words, new customer or existing customer)

The requirement above states that a 'telesales operator' – someone who phones you up from a call centre or someone who answers your call at a call centre – must ensure you are a valid customer with whatever company the operator represents. There's no explicit description of how this is done.

Step 2 asks what data might be associated with the requirement. The data would be:

> Customer name, address, phone number, account number or null, DoB

'Null' means there is no existing account number for this person; 'DoB' – date of birth.

Step 3 recommends we write these down in a table. So now we create a requirements table:

Requirement	Data
The telesales operator needs to verify the customer's current status with the company (in other words, new customer or existing customer)	Customer name, address, phone number, account number or null, DoB

Step 4 asks whether there is a process (or workflow) or similar involved? Yes, clearly the telesales operator has to use the software to input the customer's particulars and identify if the customer has an account or not. This could be a scenario or it could be a use case (see next chapter).

Step 5 asks that we document this process or create a reference to it. In our example, let's describe a potential scenario of the conversation between the operator and the customer.

Dialogue Scenario 1.2:

Customer calls about product; telesales answers the call:
Customer: 'Hello I'd like to buy the new magic fish.'
Operator: 'Jolly good, sir. Tell me, are you an existing customer?'
Customer: 'Yes, I am real.'
Operator: 'No, I mean have you bought stuff from us before? Could I have your name?'

Customer: 'I don't think I have. My name's Bill Custard.'
Operator: 'And your postcode Mr Custard?'
Customer: 'ABC 123.'
Operator: 'House number, sir?'
Customer: 'Number 4.'
Operator: 'That's 4 Railway Terrace in Plaffletown?'
Customer: 'That's correct.'
Operator: 'I see you bought something from us last year.'
Customer: 'Did I? Oh yes, I forgot, was that the chicken powder?'
Operator: 'Yes, it was, Mr Custard.'

I like to have dialogue when working on how someone like an operator will communicate with a customer. Telesales operators are typically scripted so our approach here fits. You could describe the scenario as a flow diagram or as a use case description or put it into a task scenario template. Whichever does not matter so much as the act of doing the one of them that's most appropriate to the context.

Step 6 asks about what you would like to see on the screen as a result of the requirement working. This is an output. We might see the following information:

> The Customer's details (name, address, email, for instance) and their purchase history if an existing customer.

Step 7 asks what would you need to input into the computer to ensure the results in step 6. I recommend you work on what you'd like to see on the screen before deciding the input. Knowing what you want to see will help you decide how you get to see it. Inputs for this requirement might be:

- *Customer account number*
- *Customer name and postcode*

Don't forget to update the table.

Requirement	Data	Process	Inputs	Outputs
The telesales operator needs to verify the customer's current status with the company (in other words, new customer or existing customer)	Customer name, address, phone number, account number or null, DoB	See dialogue scenario 1.2	Customer account number; Customer name and postcode	The Customer's details (name, address, email, for instance) and their purchase history if an existing customer

Step 8 adds a unique identifier to the requirement. This is giving it a number. This aids in traceability in that you ought to be able to go from the code to the specification to check the code matches the specification. Having the unique identifier just helps isolate the specific requirement whose description may be similar to others. We add a number into the first column: UR1. It is a user requirement.

ID	Requirement	Data	Process	Inputs	Outputs
UR1.	The telesales operator needs to verify the customer's current status with the company (in other words, new customer or existing customer)	Customer name, address, phone number, account number or null, DoB	See dialogue scenario 1.2	Customer account number; Customer name and postcode	The Customer's details (name, address, email, for instance) and their purchase history if an existing customer

Step 9 asks about the qualities the system should display with regard to the success of the requirement. We may need to revert to the business requirements (in whichever form these are in) to find out.

ID	Requirement	Data	Process	Inputs	Outputs	Quality
R1.	The telesales operator needs to verify the customer's current status with the company (in other words, new customer or existing customer)	Customer name, address, phone number, account number or null, DoB	See dialogue scenario 1.2	Customer account number; Customer name and postcode	The Customer's details (name, address, email, for instance) and their purchase history if an existing customer	**Speed**: existing customer record must display within 5 seconds of input of customer name and postcode if under 200 operators using system, or within 10 seconds if more than 200 operators **Reliability**: correct customer details are retrieved 99% of all cases.

In the above table you can see we are interested in speed (or timing) and reliability of our system. We have a timing requirement that the system should respond to the user inputs within certain time frames subject to how many people are using the system at the same time. Our goal is to keep our communication with customers as short but efficient as possible. There is a reliability requirement of ensuring the correct details are retrieved from the database 99 per cent of the time. We won't specific 100 per cent because if something were to go wrong, legally we would be in trouble. The unspecified 1 per cent gives us freedom from liability in this circumstance. It's a CYA principle.

Step 10 asks about the priority of this requirement. Prioritisation is key in determining which requirement to work on first. The responsibility for determining which requirement gets done when should lay with the customer unless some backend work needs to be done to support the front-end work. Normally customers do not get to see backend requirements work but they should be aware that a certain amount of architectural, interfacing (with other systems) and database work needs to be done, including ensuring security and privacy protocols are met. Priorities can take many forms: 1, 2, 3 (one high, 3 low, 2 somewhere in between). Or '0' minimum viable product, 1 as must have and so on. Or the MoSCoW approach of Must have, Should have, Could have or Won't have. It's easy to get confused between should and could. Won't implies we throw away the requirement but my view on this is we keep it in a spreadsheet until later – it's a requirement just not on this current project. I prefer the minimum viable product (MVP) approach. We only build that which we deem is vital to the product's function and hence business success. I will give the requirement we are specifying a '0' – part of the minimum viable product.

ID	Requirement	Data	Process	Inputs	Outputs	Quality	Priority
R1.	The telesales operator needs to verify the customer's current status with the company (in other words, new customer or existing customer)	Customer name, address, phone number, account number or null, DoB	See dialogue scenario 1.2	Customer account number; Customer name and postcode	The Customer's details (name, address, email, for instance) and their purchase history if an existing customer	**Speed**: existing customer record must display within 5 seconds of input of customer name and postcode if under 200 operators using system, or within 10 seconds if more than 200 operators **Reliability**: correct customer details are retrieved 99% of all cases.	0 (MVP)

What I have just described is the most basic approach to 'specification' but that has as much coverage as possible. The specification document needs to be signed off and someone needs to track progress as the project moves through its phases. Also, note that the document is a *live* document and it should be updateable at any point in the project.

As such, you should also consider:

- Who is responsible for implementing the requirement (developer)?
- Who owns the requirement (customer)?
- Do we need to constrain formats?
    - E.g. Date of birth format: DD-MM-YYYY or YY-MM-DD?
    - E.g. Length of data fields: Customer account number alphanumeric, max 4 numbers, 3 digits e.g. from 0001 AAA to 9999 ZZZ
- Other diagrams: UML, flowcharts, data model,[4] screen diagrams, etc., can add value to the specification.

Some approaches to development like to consider dependencies. A dependent requirement can be described as a requirement unable to be coded until another requirement it is dependent upon has been. Agile development does not like dependencies very much and I agree. We only consider absolutely necessary dependencies as and when we cannot avoid them any longer. It is sort of obvious that some requirements will need others to be completed to work properly in the context of the whole system. To this end, we may find that almost any function (as depicted by a requirement) will relate or depend upon almost any other. This creates a highly coupled approach to development and is not at all sensible. The one time I can see dependencies being important to work out is in a portfolio of projects where there are several development projects approved to deliver a company-wide all bells and whistles solution. In this circumstance, you may well need to thread a coherent path through the dependency (and political) tree you are creating at the project level. If the issue did arise on one project, I would then have to rethink whether to explicitly discuss dependencies. To be honest, it isn't easy to see how dependencies could be such a problem unless development teams were separated, some in e.g. Malaysia and some in the UK and some in Hungary. Dependencies would be a problem here and you'd need to coordinate with your colleagues overseas to ensure the right stuff got built in the right order.

REQUIREMENTS EXERCISE 2

Document in a specification table the requirements for the quality assurance check in the Fizzit case. You will need to look through Appendix 2 (the full Fizzit case documentation) to identify the requirements!

As ever, my solution (which may differ to yours) can be found in the Solutions Appendix 1.

Notes

1 Ian Bray, *An Introduction to Requirements Engineering* (2002), Addison Wesley. An excellent book. Ian was a mentor of mine on aspects of requirements engineering, especially problem frames, when I was a post-grad student.
2 An excellent, practical and short book on requirements in general and on workshops is: Ian Alexander, Richard Stevens, *Writing Better Requirements*, Addison Wesley 2002
3 I write about practical content analysis at length in my book *Strategic Requirements Analysis* (Routledge, 2015); please look for this information there.
4 I am avoiding data modelling in its entirety in this book. You'll find plenty of excellent text books on data modelling in bookshops, in the library and a wealth of great advice online.

Chapter 5

Use Cases

Use cases are one of the most popular requirements modelling tools. They are useful for diagramming how major functions relate to each other and to actors. Use cases focus on function rather than data flow. Use cases first appeared in software engineering in the 1990s. They became a full part of the Unified Modelling Language (UML) and the focus of many textbooks and research.[1] It isn't anywhere near an understatement to say that UML completely transformed the world of software engineering entirely. Prior to UML there were several competing object-oriented analysis and design notations. UML effectively replaced them all by unifying the works of Ivar Jacobson, Grady Booch and Jim Rumbaugh, three of the leading methodologists of their time. They ended the era of the 'methods wars', as it was called. I was originally taught Coad and Yourdon's object-oriented analysis and design when I began to study software engineering. I remember life before UML. There were so many approaches proposed and many of them very good indeed. Whether UML was the best and won out because of it is not possible to say. The history of methods and UML is not for this book but if you're interested, look it up. I recommend you do because what you'll see is that many of the techniques and tools for analysis and design that are taught today as if they are new are not really. Often, they are adaptations of techniques and tools that have been around for a very long time.

With the advent of agile development, user stories started to challenge use cases. User stories are often depicted as written onto index cards or even post-it notes. This looseness in formalism, in my view, was very useful to help discuss, analyse and organise core features. But it is nowhere near enough to build a complete system. Use cases, on the other hand, are often shown as diagrams that are ridiculously simple in appearance. Not good enough, either. There is another side to use cases that is a lot more rigorous and that is the use case description. More on this later but I would like to begin with the diagram.

Use Case Diagram

The most basic elements of a use case diagram are as follows:

Actor – someone or something that interacts with the proposed system, such as a user or a customer or an administrator. An actor 'something' might be a remote data store or a different system or a different department or organisation.

Use case – this is the transaction or feature that is going to be built. There are normally several and you should really only include such features as those that are of key value to the actor. For example, a user who wants to book a holiday via an online booking portal would view value as: book hotel, book airline, secure payment. A common use case I see in student projects is 'log in' and 'register account'. But these are a staple of almost all applications where you would book something or pay for something, you need to log in and/or register. As such, its unique value is considered a standard function of most systems and not something to include in a use case diagram. Its place would be in a requirements table.

Elements of the Use Case Diagram

The following figures are the 'typical' use case diagram elements found in most books and papers on use cases. Let's take a look at them. Imagine we want to describe an online music store where it is possible for customers to make purchases. A simple use case diagram is represented in Figure 5.1. What we see on the left is a stick figure labelled 'Customer'. This stick figure has a generic name: actor. An actor is basically a user of a system. It got the moniker of 'actor' rather than 'user', as legend would have it, from a mistranslation of the original Swedish word into English. Use cases and their usage in what was labelled 'object-oriented software engineering' (the 'OOSE' method) were created by Ivar Jacobson in Sweden prior to becoming a staple of UML. So, when you read 'actor' with regard to use cases, think of 'user' who has *direct* contact with a system. This contact is called an interaction. The interaction spans the length of a complete transaction or function: the 'use case.' In Figure 5.1

this is 'Buy music'. The line between the actor and the use case, called an association, just states that the actor can perform the use case on the system. The system is a box around the use case.

One other thing to note is that the box edge is called the system boundary. Anything inside it is going to be programmed and anything outside it isn't – at least not on this project. Users are definitely always outside the boundary. There are exceptions which we won't go into too much here but it is possible to put actors (not 'users') inside the system to represent a subsystem or a database, for instance.

Figure 5.2 expands the online store example to include a further use case 'review music' that can be performed by the Customer. There's an additional actor, Member Customer, who can also upload music. The Member Customer can also do everything the Customer can do, buy music and review music.

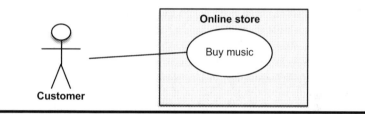

Figure 5.1   Actor, use case and system.

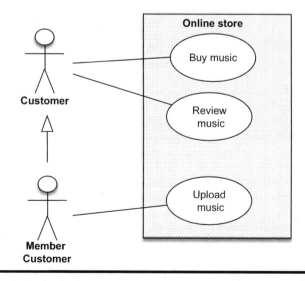

Figure 5.2   Actor specialisation.

Rather than draw association lines from the Member Customer to the review music and buy music use cases, causing a crossing on lines that would clutter the diagram, we use a white-headed triangle arrow to denote a generalisation–specialisation relationship between the actors. This concept comes from programming, called inheritance in object-oriented programming. But in the use case model it simply means that the Member Customer can do everything the Customer can do. The proviso for using this arrow is that the Member Customer must also do something else. The Member Customer *is* a Customer, plus more. The next Figure 5.3, introduces one of the complexities of the use case diagram, stereotype relationships.

Figure 5.3 shows another use case, search catalogue. This use case does not have a direct association line to an actor. Instead, there are dotted arrows coming from the buy music and review music use cases pointing to it. Both arrows have the word includes surrounded by the French speech marks << >> -- <<includes>>. These guillemets denote a stereotype. A stereotype denotes a standard type of behaviour or characteristic. The includes behaviour means that the use case steps within the search catalogue are used by *both* buy music and review music. In programming there is something called global code which tends to be functions and attributes available for use in various parts of the application. It's easier to create a global function or variable than repeat it several times, running the risk of overwriting the variable's value. Back to the use case. Both buy music and review music must search catalogue prior to completion. Rather than write long use case descriptions for

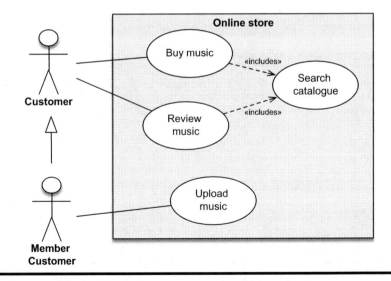

Figure 5.3   The <<includes>> stereotype.

both use cases where a significant section of the description is identical, it makes sense to effectively create a global use case and <<includes>> it. Important note: The global use case has an arrow pointing at it – not the other way around. Another important note – when you use <<includes>> there has to be more than one main use case including it. You cannot include from only one use case. In the example, there are two use cases including the search catalogue.

There is a problem with the <<extends>> stereotype that is commonly described in articles and textbooks. I will get to this and my solution to it later. But for now, it is useful for you to understand how <<extends>> works as per the book. The idea is that if there is a variation to the normal course of a use case, that is valid yet uncommon, we can <<extends>> into (interrupt) the main use case in the right place with the extension use case, which is different behaviour to the normal use case. In Figure 5.4 we can see that upload music has an extension pointing into it and this is called block overwrite. We don't really know what this means until we see the use case description, so the descriptions are something that simply cannot be ignored and are of more value to developers than the diagram. Let's consider the scenario: the Member Customer wants to upload music to the online store but has not realised there is a copy of the song already there. The block overwrite extension use case will step through a function that informs the actor the song is already there and asks whether the customer would like to proceed to upload and overwrite the existing song or to stop.

If you find your use case diagram does not have any include or extend use cases, I strongly recommend you don't bother with the diagram at

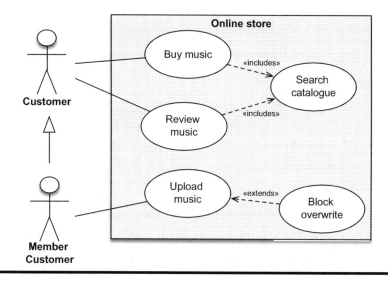

Figure 5.4   The standard <<extends>> stereotype.

Table 5.1 Tabulating Use Case Figure 5.4

Actor	Use Case	<<Includes>>	<<Extends>>
Customer	Buy music	Search catalogue	—
	Review music		
Member Customer (is a Customer)	Upload music	—	Block overwrite

all but focus on use case descriptions and the requirements table. This may be a bit of a surprise to you but the diagram has received far too much attention in comparison to the description and we can create a table instead if we wish (see Table 5.1).

If it is so simple to table a use case diagram, then do so. Having both works better. Just don't get too fixated on the diagram. Saying that, I would like you to tackle a more complex use case diagram exercise!

USE CASE DIAGRAM EXERCISE 1

This exercise is a bit more complex than the examples shown but it provides a little bit more of a realistic case and a worthwhile one to model.

A high street bank wants to create an integrated countertop bank teller system to be able to help customers with their transactions. A bank clerk can help customers by depositing cash for them and withdrawing funds from their account at their request. They can also exchange foreign currency (if it is a currency request from a country rarely used, the notes will have to be looked up to check their validity) and finally clerks can exchange small coin amounts for larger currency such as notes.

The bank also has a manager that can perform the tasks of the clerk and handle more complex transactions like approval of loans, create a new account and create a mortgage account.

The third member of staff is the mortgage advisor who can approve a loan and create a new mortgage account. To do this, the mortgage advisor needs access to the customer's bank account record in the bank's database.

There is also a terminal in the bank for customers to create new accounts which is part of the teller system. The customer can read, update and delete their existing account.

A solution is found in Solutions Appendix 1.

The Slight Problem with <<extends>>

Going back to the use case diagram approach, I've always had an issue with how <<extends>> is interpreted and therefore used over the twenty-plus years I have been applying use cases – this could just be me but I have found the way extension points has been interpreted is not universal. Different authors, academics and students treat <<extends>> differently. Generally, I advise that you don't use <<extends>> at all because it is hard to tell when you would like to interrupt the flow of a use case with the extension. Sometimes the interrupt – which would work better than extends as a stereotype i.e. <<interrupts>> – is percentage-oriented. That is, you may find the condition to interrupt the main use case is described as occurring only 5 per cent of the time and hence the use case earns the <<extends >> label. But percentages don't give enough value, for me at least, to justify the <<extends>> stereotype. I was only half-joking in reference to the <<interrupts>> stereotype. That's part of UML's flexibility. You can create your own stereotypes. I am critical of this to some degree because the more generic a tool, the less useful it is to solve a specific problem. However, in this case, maybe <<interrupts>> would work reasonably well. For example, in about 5 per cent of cases, the main use case is interrupted from its normal flow because of this circumstance so we need to add a few additional steps into the transaction. Sometimes I think the extension points is better addressed as a programming solution and that we simply need to add to the requirements document the condition as a scenario, plus whatever specification may be necessary to document. That's because extension points tend to be conditional. 'If this thing occurs then do something, else something else.' When you have to use *if...then* statements in the description, you're in pseudocode world which we can call semi-formal specification in that you're describing the behaviour of the system from an external point of view. That's fine to do but I think the UML <<extends>> doesn't make life that much better for analysts because of the potential for confusion as described above. The other thing with extensions is that the use case is expected to return back to the main use case at the step after it was interrupted (hence my feeling that <<interrupts>> is a better stereotype description). But sometimes the extension forces the use case to terminate. That is, the extension needs to do something a little unusual so cannot simply return back to the normal flow of events every time. Again, we are in the situation where we need *if... then... else...* statements. I also think about security issues and if a cyber attack is identified then the normal flow of a use case may extend as far as a system shutdown to stop a virus spreading. There's no way it can return to a normal flow at this point.

As I said, I like the idea of <<extends>> but find its execution open to interpretation. It's important that modelling elements should mean one thing only and not anything else. It's clear not everyone interprets extension points in the same way I do or anyone else. I have found that students simply get confused by this stereotype and are not sure when to use it. But they feel compelled to use it because they have been taught it or read about it. Martin Fowler, in his excellent book, *UML Distilled* (which I suggest you take a look at because it is very much the practitioner's perspective) recommends you don't bother to use <<extends>> at all. I tend to agree.

In looking back to the business process chapter, I referenced the error and cancel notation in BPMN (see Chapter 2 Figure 2.8 especially for the error notation). I really think that the BPMN error reversal notation makes a lot of sense as an extend use case. It really struck me, almost immediately, that here was a really good business example of an <<extends>> use case. It brings clarity to the concept of how and when to use an <<extends>> stereotype use case. When we look at BPMN and how we can connect ideas in models, the error symbol, representing a reversal of behaviour if a process mistake or problem arises, matches how I want to view <<extends>> in UML use cases. Much of the above section has been describing a confusion I have identified with the standard and not-so-standard interpretations of the <<extends>> use case. To make sure you don't fall into this trap, which can be unnecessarily time-consuming, I suggest that only in the situation of a BPMN diagram's usage of the error symbol should we consider that being reflected in a use case diagram via the <<extends>> notation. I recommend that in no other circumstances should you apply the <<extends>> even though I've given you examples of the 'textbook' interpretations of it. As Martin Fowler has wisely written – avoid it. So let's be a bit more formal here and state that we should:

Only use UML <<extends>> use cases (in the diagram and descriptions) <u>if and only if</u> *a business process model represents an error (see Figure 2.8, for example, in subsection 'Errors and cancellations' in Chapter 2) and the steps taken to undo that error, presuming these steps are conducted on the system to be developed. If the undo steps are manual, then no <<extends>> use case should be shown in the use case diagram or description.*

Now it is time to move on the documentation part of the use case: descriptions.

Use Case Descriptions

The use case name should be a goal, something of value a user would like to achieve through interaction with the system. A use case should also be a repeatable activity for the user as well as being of value. This, in my opinion, rules out – in most cases – typical use cases I see submitted by students in assignments such as 'log in' and 'subscribe'. Though we can argue these steps are of value and repeatable, they are also standard practice for almost all online applications at least, and log in is common for just about all business applications – if you're working in a company. I have to log in to a number of systems and applications (though not all) at my work. But this does not mean I should include 'log in' as a use case. Instead, I would consider: 'upload lecture', 'record marks', 'give class' as valuable use cases in my role as an academic.

Meta-models provide insight into how a model can be constructed, what element relates to which part and constraints by which you can create your models. The UML standard defined an extendible meta-model that you are free to extend. This is useful when you need to add new constructs such as the one we discussed above, the potential stereotype <<interrupts>>. Figure 5.5 presents a meta-model for the use case description.

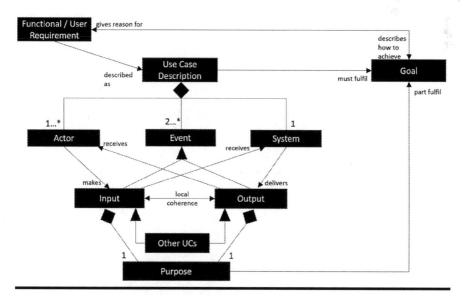

Figure 5.5 Use case description meta model. This figure is adapted from my PhD thesis, *Heuristics for Use Case Descriptions*, Bournemouth University, 2003. The writing rules presented below are also adapted from my PhD.

A use case description describes how a requirement achieves (or part achieves) a goal. The use case description must fulfil the goal to some extent. We mentioned that use case names should be valuable and repeatable goals for a user. This is one way to help ensure we are approaching the use case in the right way. The use case description is composed of a system (and we assume that one is enough in this model, not considering distributed systems), two or more events (because we expect an input with a following output at a minimum) and at least one actor (otherwise the use case cannot function as being external behaviour of the system though the actor could be another system). Inputs and outputs are kinds of events. The system receives an input and delivers an output in response. It is the actor who initiates the inputs. There should be local coherence between the input and the output. Local coherence means that one sentence logically follows from the previous. We explain this later in the style guideline 5. In Figure 5.5 we see also that other use cases (includes and extends) are types of input and output. Each input and output has a purpose (a subgoal). The sum of the subgoals should fulfil the goal of the use case in its entirety except for one thing: a measure of user satisfaction.

The below box shows an example use case description. Take a look at it and I will explain what is going on. We'll take the bank teller case as described in the use case diagram exercise above. If you've skipped ahead without having an attempt at the diagram, at least look at the diagram solution in Appendix 1 first.

UC1. DEPOSIT CASH

Actors: Customer, Bank Clerk
Trigger: Customer asks to deposit cash into account
Context: Customer arrives at counter and has asked to deposit £500 into his business account.
Pre-conditions: Customer has account; cash legal tender
Main Flow of Events:

1. The bank clerk selects access the customer account.
2. The system displays the account details.
3. The bank clerk adds £500 to the account total.
4. The account total displayed increases by £500.
5. The clerk prints a receipt for the customer.
6. The system acknowledges printed receipt.
7. The clerk ends the transaction.

Post-conditions:
The customer's account is increased by £500
Alternative Flow of Events:
    a2. The system fails to display the account details.
    a2i. Prompt clerk to check customer account number.
    a2ii. Clerk repeats step 1 in main flow.
Exception Flow of Events:
    e2. System flags problem with customer account.
    e2i. Clerk messages manager.
    e2ii. Step 7 in the main flow.

We'll now go through the use case description line by line.

UC1. This is the unique identifier for the use case. Imagine you are developing a very large system where there are around 100 use cases. You need to keep track of which screen functions relate to which use case in the requirements. One way to help this is to document in the requirements which use case(s) are referred to. The designer uses the requirements to inform on the interfaces of the system. Including a unique identifier for each use case makes it much easier to track down which requirement relates to which use case. If you only included the use case name, it would take up more space. In a spreadsheet application you would include the use case identifier and use it as a hyperlink to the actual use case description document.

Use case name: Deposit cash. The use case name should represent a goal for the user. In this case, it is to deposit cash. The name is written as a verb-noun phrase: 'Do something.' The use case name is also quite short as two words. This is typically long enough to give the goal or name of the use case and for it to make sense. If you have a long name – more than three words – then it is likely you are unclear what the goal of the user is. Take another look at the requirements to help clarify this.

Actor(s): Customer, Bank Clerk. In actual fact, I don't need to include the Customer as an actor because there is no direct interaction with the system by the Customer. But the problem with this is that the requirement is about the Customer and for the Customer, so to exclude the Customer would mean the risk of not building the right focus into the system. We have included the Customer in the Context of the use case description also. I would always err on the side of inclusion because if you stick only with the direct actor – as per the rules of use case modelling – some of the wider context and understanding is lost.

Trigger: Customer asks to deposit cash into account. A trigger is the mechanism by which the use case can commence. Triggers originate in business process modelling and have the purpose of being the required thing that 'forces' the process to commence. In this case, a Customer has approached the bank teller window and asked the bank clerk to deposit some cash into an account.

Context: Customer arrives at counter and has asked to deposit £500 into his business account. The context in use case descriptions is an attempt to appear more scenario in intent. The reason for this is that use case descriptions, as you have just read, are somewhat system focussed – everything in it refers to a usage of the system. Context allows you to include more information to ground the use case in.

Pre-conditions: Customer has account; cash legal tender. The pre-condition(s) tend to refer to the state the system should be in to permit the use case to function. I personally prefer to be a little more abstract than just looking at the system workings. Natural pre-conditions are that the customer does have a registered account at the bank and that the cash isn't out of circulation (it's too old) or counterfeit. Note that trigger coupled with context can appear to cover very similar ground. You use what is good for you in your own context but typically we see triggers and pre-conditions. Context is a bonus if you find it. I like context because it provides a little more real world thinking about the system.

Main Flow of Events. This is the point at which we include the normal interactions between the Actor and the System. This is sometimes called the 'happy day scenario' where the most typical and successful interaction is described until the use case is complete. The numbered steps constitute the main interactions. Step 1 is a bit different to the others because it has underlined text. This denotes an includes or an extends use case. It's underlined to show this and also permits the analyst to hyperlink to the appropriate use case description. The way in which the steps make sense together (input -> response; input -> response....) are an implementation of use case description writing rules, which are described below in detail. Step 7 is important because it concludes the use case appropriately. I use the words more precisely than you think. I could have written:

Clerk closes the account

Use case ends.

But this could be misinterpreted as closing the customer's account permanently so the customer would no longer have access to it. We realise this would be wrong but it is easy to write such a sentence and have this sentence remain in the use case through to implementation. At its worst, a developer may interpret this to mean: build a function to allow the Clerk to shut down the customer's account. We don't want this to happen at all, of course. Some consideration – and walkthrough with colleague(s) and customer representatives if available – would spot this.

Post-conditions: The customer's account is increased by £500. The post-condition should indicate the state of the system or part of the system once the use case is complete. This is related to business processes where you can show the state of the process. For use cases, it is useful to make the post-condition relevant to the use case itself. In our example, I show that the customer's account amount has changed by the amount deposited. The state of the system could have been described by writing something like: *The system is ready for the next transaction.* It would be correct to do so but I think it should be clear that the system ought to be ready for the next transaction at the close of the use case. Perhaps I am being loose with the rules of use case descriptions here but I prefer not to overload the reader with some things we take as a given.

Alternative Flow of Events:

> *a2. The system fails to display the account details.*
> *a2i. Prompt clerk to check customer account number.*
> *a2ii. Clerk repeats step 1 in main flow.*

Use alternative flows of events when a situation arises commonly but is not the normal flow of events. In this case, a2 (a = alternative; 2 = number of the step in main flow), the system did not respond to the input in step 1. Steps a2i and a2ii are a mini-use case to address this alternative flow. It is normally the case that the clerk did not input the bank account correctly. These days clerks will swipe a bank card and this alternative would be different. Step a2ii would say: reswipe bank card. Once the alternative flow is finished, we return to the main use case.

Exception Flow of Events:

> *e2. System flags problem with customer account.*
> *e2i. Clerk messages manager.*
> *e2ii. Step 7 in the main flow.*

Exceptional flows of events represent valid but uncommon behaviour. In our example, the exceptional flow is at the main flow step 2 again and this is checking the account. In this case, we see that there is a problem with the customer account. We cannot resolve the problem (which could be perfectly valid) so step e2i has the clerk call the manager. It's an issue for the manager to address otherwise the clerk would have been able to fix it here. It may be that a different form of identification is required to enable the account – it could be a new one. There may have been some suspicious activity on the account and the manager needs to confirm this with the customer. These are beyond our interests but important to flag. The exception ends the use case by ending the transaction.

This is a fairly typical use case description. There are many templates available including a two-column format for the main flow, one column for the actor and one for the system. I don't really like this approach but it does enforce input -> response.

Do you need to always include alternative and exceptional events? No, but it is common to include the most obvious. I prefer to include exceptional flows because these can flag potential security issues. Alternative flows can be taken out of the main use case and documented as use case scenarios. These would include much of the template but with the alternative steps rather than the main flows. The alternative flows would become more main flows. You would need to alter the use case name to indicate the alternative flow you are writing about. I avoid use case scenarios because they add a lot more effort to your already heavy workload. But if there is a really important alternative, for example, two clearly valid and common threads to achieve the same use case goal, then you need to write the alternative and make sure the document's reader is aware of this.

Testing the use case is done by ensuring all the steps are relevant to the use case goal (name of the use case) and that you've listed all the relevant actors, pre- and post-conditions, triggers and context. You can do this by stepping through the use case description with:

1. Yourself
2. A colleague (analyst or manager)
3. A user and/or customer representative

You agree before you commence to look for specific issues (e.g. actors listed but not used, pre- and post-conditions that are sensible to the use case, alternative flows whose numbering is aligned to main flow steps and so on). Read the use case description and flag where you identify a specified issue. You can agree to fix it then and there or if there is uncertainty (e.g. step in the main flow seems to be wrong) you need to check with the stakeholders (customers, managers, users, developers). These tests should be part of an official document walkthrough or review. It's important to document the test occurred and that changes are agreed and the use cases updated.

Now we have discussed a use case description in terms of its components, we should look at an important set of rules for writing the use cases.

Use Case Description Writing Rules

Use case descriptions have been published in all shapes and sizes, as paragraphs of text, as two columns, as pseudocode and as bullet-point lists. I prefer to write use case descriptions following a logical structure. We begin by examining elements of style.

Seven Style Rules

Style 1: placement of events
Each sentence in the description should be on a new, numbered line. Alternatives and exceptions should be described in a section below the main description and the sentence numbers should agree. For example:

Main Flow:
   1. The patient record appears on the screen.
   2. The doctor enters the patient's new address.

Alternative Flow:
   a1. The doctor enters the patient's new mobile phone number.

Style 2: present tense
All sentences are in present tense format. The use case should describe actions and events in the here and now, not the past or future. For example:

The operator <u>presses</u> the button.
The checkout <u>displays</u> the amount payable.

Style 3: keep the sentences simple!
Avoid using adverbs and adjectives. These add unnecessary clutter and are hard to quantify. Only use negatives in alternative and exceptional flows of events. Avoid pronouns (e.g. he, she, it, we, their etc.). Examples of over-complexity:

The doctor writes the prescription <u>slowly</u>. (adverb not needed).
The patient swallows the <u>big</u> pill. (adjective not needed).

The patient stands next to the doctor.
<u>He</u> puts the prescription in <u>his</u> pocket. (who is 'he' and whose 'pocket' is it?)

Style 4: give explanations <u>and</u> data

Use cases are function or even process-oriented. But you need to capture data to explain things in more detail. Place explanations in brackets ():

> The librarian enters the borrower's details
> (details are: name, address, phone number, email, library card number)

Style 5: logical local coherence

The sentence you are writing now should refer to something in the previous sentence if possible. It helps in understanding the use case. For example:

> 1. The cat sits on the <u>mat</u>.
> 2. The <u>mat</u> is in Fred's kitchen.

The mat in (2) coheres to the mat in sentence (1).

The meta model in Figure 5.5 shows there should be local coherence between inputs and outputs. Hopefully, style rule 5 has explained what this means.

Style 6: coverage meaning action -> logical response

When an action occurs in a description, there should be an immediate meaningful response documented, or a response somewhere to that action in the same use case. This helps with coverage–we don't miss things. For example:

> 1. The doctor enters the patient's record identification number.
> 2. The system displays the patient's record.

Style 7: underline other use case names

When we include a use case or are extended into by another use case, just write the name of the use case and underline it. This is also useful in terms of including hyperlinks to the other use cases – you can jump straight there to read that description. An example:

> The user makes a <u>new equipment request</u>.

> The example use case description above included an underlined use case in step 1.

Two Structure Rules

There are also two rules on the grammatical structure of each event or sentence.

Structure 1: subject verb object

Identified as the most common occurring use case event description.

The operator presses the button.

Structure 2: subject *verb object prepositional phrase*

The operator gives the tool **to the mechanic**.
The builder puts the bricks **on top of the pile of rubbish**.
The system reminds the operator **to save all the open files**.

The **bold** text are examples of prepositional phrases.

USE CASE DESCRIPTION EXERCISE 2

Write a use case description for the use case Buy Music in Figure 5.4.
Don't forget to use the template elements appropriately – see the
  example description.
Also, don't forget to apply the use case description writing rules.
You can find my answer in the Solutions Appendix 1.

We need to think about deriving potential use cases from a business
process model and from problem frames. The following Table 5.2 follows the pattern we have established in previous chapters.

Table 5.2 Linking Use Cases with BPMN, Problem Frames and Requirements

BPMN Element	Problem Frame Element/ Requirement	Use Case Element	Explanation
Pool, Swimlane	Domain of interest, Machine (possibly)	Actor, system if machine domain	This is relatively easy to work out. If the BPMN pool/swimlane is a person, then it can be a use case actor.
Task	Requirement	Use case (possibly)	It's possible for BPMN task actions to be use cases if there are user tasks where the user uses the system. In problem frames a task can be a requirement. Whether the requirement is a use case is another matter.

(Continued)

Table 5.2 (Continued) Linking Use Cases with BPMN, Problem Frames and Requirements

BPMN Element	Problem Frame Element/ Requirement	Use Case Element	Explanation
Message	Connection between domains	Use case (possibly)	It's possible a message could come from a person in BPMN to a system. This could be viewed as a use case. I don't think of shared phenomena as use cases because of the clash of granularity (the level of detail we need to look at something e.g. an engine or the individual components of the engine viewed together?)
Error task	Requirement	<<Extends>> use case	This is our only reason to depict <<Extends>> stereotypes in the use case diagram – and subsequent descriptions.
Actions within tasks, timers, decision gateways	Requirements, specification	Use case (possibly)	Elements of BPMN that are doing things can be functional requirements and constraints on behaviour of the system (which are part of requirements specification, basically) and could be modelling with use cases.

To be perfectly honest, I lumped problem frames and requirements together because we don't really need to compare with problem frames. It would be sufficient to connect BPMN and use cases. Use cases can be derived from requirements or descriptions of features of a system we imagine using. Problem frames are a topic that stands alone in many ways. Jackson, who created problem frames, isn't a big fan of use cases. Because business processes are process or step-centric, they are a better fit with use cases, which are also step-centric. If I were in a hurry on a project, which would be normal, I might not consider using problem frames simply because they take time to do. I would explicitly spend time with the business concept model, business processes, requirements and then think about use cases. If I had time, I would put problem frames in between because they are so structural in nature and not at all procedural. The nature of the project would also shape my decision. If the project were very data centric, then use cases may not be used as heavily – I would want to focus more on structure, understanding the problem domain through problem frames – or just the requirements as they are.

Note

1 There have been probably hundreds of books published on UML over the years. I still think the best are by the 'Three Amigos', the original creators of UML: Grady Booch, Ivar Jacobson and James Rumbaugh. They wrote three excellent guides on using UML. My favourite is *The Unified Modeling Language User Guide*. There is also the formal specification that is updated every now and again by the object management group: https://www.omg.org/spec/UML/2.5.1/PDF

Chapter 6

A Brief Discussion
of Software Project
Management

Thus far in this book I haven't had a great deal of opportunity to discuss project management in general so now will do so, if you will indulge me. Notice in the chapter title I include 'software' before project management. The reason for this is that software development isn't quite the same as property development (or engineering projects either), so project management for property ought to be different to project management for software. Strange then, that in the early days of software project management, the basic management approach was the same as for property. The problem with this is that it's relatively straightforward to work out the number of bricks required to build a house, the length of wiring, the number of roof tiles, the plumbing and sewage systems, the doors, windows, house frames and all the rest. Why? Because when you build one house, you build ten or twenty or a hundred that are all the same. There's no need for wastage, therefore. You know the optimal number of people and their required skill set. They know what to do without too many questions. You know how long it takes to build one house so you multiply that by ten or twenty or a hundred. It's that simple. There aren't that many variations to a house either; the roof is on top, doors open and close, windows are see-through and water goes down plug holes. Don't get me wrong, building a house is not easy. But by following the tried and tested methods of doing so, one that's been

DOI: 10.1201/9781003168119-6

around for a really long time, there's really little excuse for getting it wrong if you're a builder.

Software projects should be the same but it isn't like building a house. It is the case that when a programme is complete and it works, it is then mass sold either as a download or it's burned on a CD. The same blueprint or code is imprinted on each disk or forms part of each download. This isn't the same thing as actually constructing ten houses that have the same architectural structure and blueprint (although 3D printing is now making houses in the USA!). Yet, the first management approaches deployed on software were similar to the building industry approach. No wonder, then, that software projects went wrong so regularly. A property development (not referring to individuals building their dream home) is a massive development of uniformity, even if the houses have slightly different configurations. A prescriptive management approach works in these circumstances (prescriptive management, in my view is: always do A first, then always do B next, then always C next and so on, where A, B, C and so on are pre-determined and recognised activities that are always successful). Software is different because: customers change their minds, the designers and developers don't have the same vision for the project, programming in the uncertainty of ongoing and irregular, and seemingly irrational, change does not lend itself to prescriptive management (though if we watch *Grand Designs* on TV, we might think this is how all houses are built!). Testing software finds all kinds of faults but misses more until it's too late; houses are tested for leaks, for instance, but they don't normally fall over. Software does. When the property is all polished and sparkling ready for show and purchase, you don't often get the customer ask for the front to be taken off and done differently. You do with software. Or the back or the sides. So why would software projects expect success when one of the mainstays of project success is flawed to begin with; that is, the project management approach selected to manage the project is not fit for purpose. OK, so why does this book recommend some of its techniques then? A good question. It all comes down to where you are in your knowledge (Which is really knowing without the experience of doing, hence 'know'ing on the 'ledge'. It's parked on the shelf until you get the experience. Then it becomes knowing.) against practical experience?

Students need a lot of structure in their studies otherwise it's very easy to be overwhelmed by the many seemingly disparate subjects that you are taught. Subjects range from learning about the history of IT to learning about how to programme in C++. That's a pretty broad subject matter and it is simply too much at times for students. Here's where project management the way it is presented in this book goes well. It matches the student experiences in classes by providing a frame for which to tie the stems of the other subjects to. I also do not promote a prescriptive do-it-by-the-numbers approach. What I am proposing is more dynamic.

Management and Requirements

It's interesting to note that there are more project management approaches on the market than there are approaches to designing software, at least to the point where the design approach is sufficiently mainstream. Project management seems to keep evolving whereas software design is rather static. I suppose this is down to the fact that software is software and in the end it is how it is programmed (object oriented or procedural or whatever else) is all that matters.

The world of requirements analysis, though, has followed a similar path of project management in that there are a lot of approaches out there for gathering requirements and there are several notations for modelling requirements. But there is a lot of stability here, too. Today's popular domain of user experience/usability engineering is a lot like the world of HCI of 25 years ago. The world of scenarios that I researched into when I did my PhD (which was a brilliant world, by the way) was ultimately usurped by the mainstream use case modelling world. Today's user stories appeared over 20 years ago (in XP) as a move against prescriptive UML modelling. All these modelling approaches are still around. No matter how we might vary them, they are basically the same as they ever were. High-fidelity prototyping is an advance because the tools available for their development are much better than they used to be. But in the end, we've moved from hand-drawn sketches to very block-like screen mock-ups to high-fidelity prototypes. Not much has changed in 25 years except the mechanism of representation. I used 'dynamic' storyboarding in building a product in my job at NICTA 15 years ago. The tools now, though, are far superior to then, and the results far more realistic than they used to be.

Lest you think this is me knocking or mocking the modern versions of existing tools (I mean by tool, a diagram type as much as I mean an electronic design aid), what I would like to say is that the field that was just emerging when I got into it is now stable and that's because it works. The tools are fit-for-purpose and this is why they are still around. And that is good. I liked the scenario world much more than use cases when I studied them in the last century. I am glad they are still here. But this is a chapter that's meant to discuss project management and present you with a few tools that will help you in your projects.

Project management is somewhat like requirements management in terms of long-term usage of the same techniques and tools. But unlike the requirements world, many of the project management tools simply don't work or at best appear to work more by luck than judgement. But for you, the target audience, we won't really be discussing those aspects too much. What am I referring to? Primarily, I am referring to most approaches for calculating project effort estimates pre-Agile. Some of these approaches were extremely influential but were never particularly accurate. Function point estimation is one such approach. Another, counting thousands of lines of code (to guess at the size of the product and divide it by a productivity number to calculate the amount of code that was writeable in a day per person on average, for instance) to give an estimate of how long it might take to complete the project. How can you count lines of code to estimate how many lines of code you need to write without having first written the lines of code? At which point, your project is already almost done! So, it's too late. You could take a sample and extrapolate based on your judgement and experience. But couldn't you simply take a best guess without having to write a lot of code first? However inaccurate some of these 'parametric' tests, as they are called, were, you may well get to learn some anyway because they are still occasionally used here and there.

Agile estimation initially tried to piggyback off the mathematical approach (Scrum did in its early days) but over time it became clear that these estimation approaches simply did not work. So now agile proposes things like 'story days' as an estimate: how many days might it take to build this user story as a vertical slice through the system? How do we get a reasonable number? We look at our project data from previous projects or even this one and search for similar functions we might have built before. How long did that one *actually* take? Three days, it says in my previous project data. OK, so our estimate for this new function, which is pretty similar, is three days. But there are some things that are different so we over-estimate and add another two days just to make sure.

One of the most difficult estimation tasks was to come up with a seriously good number. To make it even more unlikely to do so, the project manager was often left to work it all out. But the agile way says to let the developer, the coder, determine the estimate. The developer is the one with experience and will actually build the function so why not get the estimate from the expert? You wouldn't ask an architect to estimate how much a renovation would cost builders to do. You'd ask the builder. And the builder would use the plans drawn up by the architect, plans that had been through the building regulations approval process and that had any structural calculations added by an expert structural engineer. After all this, the estimate would be pretty accurate to the actual, all things being equal.

So why not do the same with project estimates--ask the experts? It seems so obvious and to be honest, a decent manager would always go to the developers for input. But most of the calculating would be done by the project manager. Well, what's wrong with the project manager doing the estimates? After all, the manager does work on the project, does get to communicate with the client and is in charge of the project team. The reason why the manager should not do any estimation (other than gather the estimates and collate them) is because the manager's job is to ensure things get done in the right order, that the team are happy or at least not rebelling and that the client and/or senior management are kept in the loop, and sometimes in the dark! The project manager doesn't cut any code, doesn't do any design work but may well do a lot of the analysis assuming a dual role on the project. Analysis, as you have seen in the other chapters, is about representing the problem to be solved in such a way as to present a potential solution in the form of models and tables.

Management, ultimately, comes down to one simple thing: motivation. A great manager is a great motivator. To motivate, a manager needs to be a confident communicator. To be a confident communicator, a manager needs to be able to present a way forward in a coherent way. To coherently present a way forward, a manager needs a good plan. To get a good plan, a manager needs to work with his or her team to get there. This journey is the most valuable part of management in the end. A plan is fine but has very little power over the destiny of a project without the team experiencing that process, and without the manager being that great motivator.

The Idea

The premise of this book is that it makes sense to combine business/requirements analysis with project management. There are a number of genuinely important reasons to think this sensible. First, projects without requirements always fail because there's no notion of what it is the software is meant to achieve. Second, projects without management always – or nearly always! – fail because there's no structure or organisation of the work needed to build the product in the right way. The requirements might be perfect but the development team needs to be organised, even if this is an agile project where developers can be as close to autonomous as possible. Someone needs to watch over them and make sure the right product is being built at the right time and in the right way. In this sense, nothing much has changed in the world of software development ever.

Nonetheless, software projects have a long history of failure. You might find this surprising giving all the gadgets and tech we have these days and in how we've allowed the technologists to dictate how we live our lives. We've openly invited the use of technology into every single aspect of our lives. There is almost nothing left in life that is not in some way controlled or affected by software, systems and technology. Even football (soccer) is now under the spell of (and undermined by, in my opinion) the VAR system!

What's the Official Record of Software Projects?

This depends upon the management approach taken. In my view, the most obvious causes of failure are those already indicated: poor requirements, poor management:

Poor requirements = poor management = project failure

because you can't successfully manage a project where the requirements are continually changing or are wrong, missing, duplicated everywhere and so on. That's why it makes sense to combine these two disciplines a bit more closely.

The fact is that projects can fail for all sorts of reasons. Top of the list are:

1. Poor requirements analysis. In fact, this isn't so much just poor work. For strategic projects, *adequate* requirements analysis – doing it by the numbers – also leads to project failure. You have to be really, really good and on the ball, all the time.
2. Scope creep. This is when, even if a project starts well and requirements are well defined, and on top of this management is going well, projects can still go wrong because of failing to keep track of added requirements and/or context. Context here means, for instance, a new group of stakeholders, or even an individual key stakeholder. Stakeholders are people or organisations that have a stake in the project, either because they are funding it or are the end users or even the project team.
3. Management not in tune with the reality of the project. Often, projects can take on a life of their own and the project manager, if he or she isn't careful, finds that the plan and schedule look a lot

different from the reality. The good news here is if the manager has spotted this, there's a great chance of saving the day. The big problem occurs when the manager hasn't spotted this and is following the plan drawn up long ago, oblivious to the actual state of the project. I was once told this is similar to the Swedish army map rule. The analogy goes like this: if you are parachuted into unknown terrain but were told before jumping out of the plane, you will be 'here' when looking at your map (an 'x' is marked on the map) but you notice the lay of the land is very different when you touch down, do you: 1. Believe in the map regardless or 2. Accept the map is wrong ('x' does not mark he spot) and go with the terrain? If you choose 1, then you might be a theorist who believes the theory even when the evidence is contrary and different. If you choose 2, then you're more a pragmatist. I prefer as a manager someone who is a pragmatist when it is required. Though it might not seem possible that managers would stick to the wrong plan, it happens.

Projects fail for a lot of reasons and often it is because several negative things occurred on your project. Narciso Cerpa and June Verner[1] (June was my manager for 5 years in Australia) explored a lot of projects and found that the main causes of software project failure were due to combinations of project management failure (e.g. poor estimation, focussing only on tiny tasks) combined with poor business analysis (e.g. missing key stakeholders and not understanding the business rationale for the project, losing sight of business objectives) as well as technical struggle (coding reveals misunderstood or missing requirements and functions). Interestingly, they found that most organisations did not think it urgent to resolve why their projects kept failing at an alarming rate. They just assumed this was normal in software development. This is baffling considering the cost of project failure. Some estimates from a few years ago: IT project failure in the US cost companies up to $150 billion every year. Yes, that's billion. In 2004, IT project failure cost 142 billion euros in the European Union.[2] A 2017 Project Management Institute report[3] identified that 14 per cent of IT projects fail in their entirety (delivered absolutely nothing). The PMI reports on projects that partially succeeded (i.e. delivered something but nothing like a complete product): 31 per cent of projects didn't meet all of their goals, 43 per cent exceeded their initial budgets massively, and 49 per cent were late by an order of magnitude. The report is entitled, *Success Rates Rising*. This should give you a clue as to the track record of IT project success!

What's the Point of Project Management?

Many students don't really get project management and even though it could be relatively easy, they find it laborious and even difficult. So I try to make it more fun and to make it more relevant to them. A lot of computer science students come to my lectures – and always come to the lectures – but struggle with the assessment. I think it has been because I tended to give too much information and students couldn't relate – through lack of experience – to why project management was even a discipline on their degree!

I get it. I studied software engineering and found management the most obtuse of the topics I took: programming in C and C++, SQL and databases; requirements analysis and systems design pre-UML, I was taught Coad and Yourdon OOA&D!; systems architecture; and then there was project management. My experience of classes was to sit with my peers and listen to the lecturer tell stories about projects he had been on, as well as teaching dull topics like the Capability Maturity Model. I actually enjoyed it because I enjoyed the stories. My peers were not so happy about it. But I still found it tricky to link project management to anything else we were doing. It was only in group mini-projects that ran for one week solid (no other classes) that I first got a little flavour of what management was actually about.

It isn't until you have to manage a project, even a student project, that you 'get' project management. Without doing a project, none of it makes sense. You can cut code in programming, even the most basic problems, and see the result. You can even design an entity relationship diagram in databases and wax lyrical on the merits of third-normal form and how your diagram meets the requirements. A UML diagram can be reasoned about in the same way. Lo-fidelity prototypes the same, too. You can even discuss a requirements table in light of the context of a business process or problem description. But a project plan? A Gantt chart? A critical path calculation? It's hard to justify project plans without a project. There seems to be something not quite technical about it. These days the Trello Kanban board is a popular tool.[4] It's actually rather good when all its features are used. However, Kanban's not an easy way to manage a project because it appears somewhat unstructured and even disorganised. But as it is popular, it tends to get thrust at students and they are told: use it because industry uses it. Industry does use it but nonetheless you've got to know how to use it properly. On a project management module on a computer science degree, this may not happen. I've done it though: thrust Trello at students, given a brief introduction to its features and told them to get on with it. But it doesn't tell you how to map out a project from the start. You need to do some management work before you Trello.

Rather than: 'here's Trello, I hope you like it,' I would rather introduce some principles of project management that make analysis and subsequent development more integrated and understandable. When you are really new to software development, which I define as *the management, analysis, design, coding and delivery of software that follows recognised principles and practices and meets the needs of the customer*, then you need some structure. Hence, the point of this text, the combination of analysis and management, to give more credence to the value of each by demonstrating the need for each other. And consequently, in the delivery of projects and products that meet your needs. Notice the definition begins with management. It has to because otherwise there is chaos. Projects and project teams that operate in a state of chaos regularly fail to succeed.

Project Management Tools of You

I've found three really useful tools for students. There's the Gantt chart (Chapter 8), which is the traditional project manager's core tool. There's the new(ish) kid on the agile block: the Kanban board (I told you I like the Trello tool!) and there's something before all this that is agnostic in terms of whether it is agile or traditional, though it is part of the traditional process, and that is the product breakdown structure. We'll look at Kanban a bit later in the book (Chapter 9). This is where project management and requirements analysis can work together. I will get to linkage in time but for now let me introduce you to the vagaries and brilliance of the product breakdown structure (next chapter).

But...before We Move On

Balance is something worth thinking about now. The first half of the book, which addresses the business–requirements aspect, has five main parts to it: business concept models, business process models, problem frames, requirements documents and use cases. That's quite a bit but then it does cover from the real-life business view (as opposed to an IT-masquerading-as-business view that you might find if you took, for instance, an object-oriented analysis/domain modelling viewpoint) to the purely IT view. All this is needed to understand the requirements that the business needs to impose or deploy the system successfully.

Project management, on the other hand, is solely about managing the construction project to the point where the IT works as it is hoped it would. Not that project management is small in scope. Not at all. But it really only places a structure around the work of construction so that work can be done in an orderly fashion. There are a lot of project management tools out there to assist in placing work in the right order. Let's take a look at a (non-exhaustive) list.

Traditional PM Tool	Brief Description	Included in Book?
Product breakdown structure (PBS)	A way of organising the main pieces of the product to be designed and built. Can include project management deliverables.	Yes
Product flow diagram	Ordering of PBS deliverables into order by which they should be built	No
Activity network diagram	Identifying and ordering of tasks needed to be done to complete the building of deliverables identified in PBS, following the basic order of the product flow diagram.	No
Critical path analysis	Way of calculating the longest path through the activity network diagram and claiming those specific activities on the critical path must be built according to their estimated duration to avoid project overrun.	No
Resource allocation	Placing roles such as 'designer' or 'database developer' onto activities identified and describing these in a different table.	No
Gantt chart	Culmination of all of the above in one place.	Yes
Estimation techniques	Techniques range from mathematical to guess work in estimating the duration of the project.	No

Agile PM Tool	Brief Description	Included in Book?
Product backlog	A list or post-it note list of main features to be built.	Yes (as part of Kanban)
Sprint backlog	The decomposition of a feature into main software tasks and listed in a table.	No
Burndown chart	The mapping of actual effort vs ideal effort in a sprint, documented in a chart.	No
Kanban board	A whiteboard or electronic version that plots progress of work items as identified in product backlog (and specified into work unit tasks)	Yes

You'll have noted that the Agile PM tool list looks a lot shorter. I could have included estimation and resource allocation too but as they are already on the first table, I didn't want to repeat myself. Though we will look into resource allocation, we are only going to do so in terms of the teams you will need to form for projects during your studies. The way you will allocate work will be how agile tends to: you choose what you want to do. That's the best way so long as all the work is covered and everyone has a fairly even share of the load. I didn't want to list the agile 'methods': Scrum, XP and so on because they all use more-or-less the same three tools at the top of the agile list. Some are employing a Kanban board more than they used to.

I am going to combine the three tools I have ticked 'Yes' to in the above tables: product breakdown structure, Gantt chart and Kanban board into a project management approach driven by and effectively designed by the requirements. The connections were briefly addressed in the Introduction to the book, in which it is stated that the Product Breakdown Structure and the Problem Frames approach have a connection. They both show main products to be made and place them in a structure, one useful for project management purposes, the other for requirements and architecture. The following table elaborates on these connections.

PM Tool	Reqts Tool	Connection
Product breakdown structure (PBS)	Problem frame diagram (PF)	The PBS lists deliverables that need to be produced in the project and it focusses mostly on software system deliverables but at a level of abstraction above atomic requirements, instead relying upon major features. The PF is similar in that it depicts what must be built and what type of product we are addressing. Its diagrammatic focus is on main features and not atomic requirements unless of high importance or core to the finished product. In combination, both identify major things (products) that need to be built. If using one (e.g. PBS) it can be considered sensible to think about how a PF would order what it needs to describe and use that order in a PBS. This is explained in Chapter 7.
Gantt chart	Requirements table	The Gantt chart maps out the main requirements to be built and in a specific order. Thus, the linkage between the requirements table and the Gantt chart is quite strong and has always been thus. More on this in Chapter 8.
Kanban board	Requirements	Kanban specifies its main features/requirements (called work items) into finer detailed chunks which then progress across the board as tasks. The Kanban board is described in Chapter 9.

Why have both the Gantt chart and the Kanban board? The Gantt chart provides the overall structure to the project, the bigger picture that agile does not present well. Agile is excellent at the detailed running of the project, which the Gantt chart isn't. Students need that bigger picture to see where they should be going and by when. But to do the actual work, a Kanban board is much more conducive to how students work together in groups. They can much more easily take a task and work it through across the board, seeing the results quickly. If you only use a Gantt chart, you can get stuck in that world of doing all the analysis, then doing all the design and then doing all the coding and running out of time! Kanban boards give students the hope they can succeed and the means by which they can demonstrate this to themselves. We staff don't need convincing – it's the students who need the encouragement and they can give it to themselves much more easily by working a main feature across a Kanban board, once specified, being guided by the product breakdown structure, task breakdown, use cases and their descriptions.

Why Not Just Propose Scrum?

Well, I did. Sort of. For final-year individual student projects, I proposed an individual Scrum-inspired method for students to get to grips with their projects[5] in the details and getting to programming much sooner than a waterfall-oriented Gantt chart offers. Plus, Gantt charts are harder to maintain. You could just do 'Scrum' but how do you link all the business analysis in? You could do 'Kanban' all by itself and ignore the product breakdown structure and Gantt chart. But you'll miss the bigger view a Gantt chart gives and you'll maybe not be able to structure your solution so well without linking problem frames to a product breakdown.

I am proposing what I am simply because I've seen enough commercially to know that if you ignore the real business issues and don't map out the processes, you'll almost always not succeed. In terms of what to teach students, I have found that the three project management tools described in this book give students all they really need for a student project to succeed. If this were a real business with a real project, I would add some estimation techniques, those to work out work-in-progress limits and estimated durations for Kanban and earned value analysis to assess current project status and future progress. Risk would be looked at, too. But these are well described elsewhere so I won't touch upon them here. I do teach them in my project management classes, so sign up if you would like to know more!

Notes

1 N. Cerpa and J. Verner (December 2009), Why did you project fail? *Communications of the ACM*, https://doi.org/10.1145/1610252.1610286
2 Business Journal (Feb 7 2012), The Cost of Bad Project Management, https://news.gallup.com/businessjournal/152429/cost-bad-project-management.aspx
3 PMI (2017), 9th Global Management Survey: Success Rates Rising, https://www.pmi.org/-/media/pmi/documents/public/pdf/learning/thought-leadership/pulse/pulse-of-the-profession-2017.pdf?sc_lang_temp=en
4 www.trello.com
5 K. Cox (2017), *Managing Your Individual Computing Project: An Agile Approach for Students and Supervisors -- 2nd Edition*, CreateSpace Publishing, ISBN: 978-1542778114.

Chapter 7

Product Breakdown Structure

The focus of this chapter is the product breakdown structure (PBS), a mainstay of traditional project planning. In this age of agile – or hybrid agile – it may be odd to promote traditional methods. In some cases, they work very well. Traditional affords time to consider structure, sequence and process in a more coherent way than agile, which is ultimately built upon the success and failure of traditional project management and the software development lifecycle (SDLC). Even though students are keen to get into agile, they need a baseline understanding of the process of planning a project in order to 'get' agile. As such, I still think there is a great deal of benefit in learning the basics of traditional planning.

The way to create a PBS is to work with the requirements primarily. You need good requirements in order to build the product to the satisfaction of the client. We've looked at different requirements techniques earlier. We need to think about two things: function and structure. Function comes from requirements and structure comes from not only the requirements but from business models and problem frames.

Basic Process and How to Get It Wrong

There is a simple process to creating a PBS. There are also some pitfalls, too. The basic process focusses on requirements and I will describe an

DOI: 10.1201/9781003168119-7

example below. But first, the pitfalls. There is a general idea that the PBS should follow the steps of the waterfall lifecycle. These steps are:

1. Requirements
2. Design
3. Coding
4. Testing
5. Deployment

Plus – sometimes – Management. The idea is to then name all the products from each phase of this SDLC. Products from the requirements phase could be: problem description, requirements tables, specification tables, stakeholder list, security requirements list, physical requirements for specific devices. We could even include the other requirements tools described in this book: business concept model, business process model, problem frames analysis, use case models. The design phase might include an entity relationship diagram, screen designs such as low-fidelity and high-fidelity prototypes, object-oriented design, a whole range of UML-oriented designs, network designs, architecture and so on. The coding phase has various elements around programming, units of code, database code, screen implementation. Testing would include creating test scripts from a test strategy, test results plus recommendations from those results. Deployment includes user training and whatever installation work is needed. The management 'phase', as it were because management does not cease until the project is over, could include a number of products. There is the contract, the planning documentation and other considerations such as risk plans, and even products such as accounts and personnel documents. It's easy to create this PBS because all you do is include all of the above in a list. The project manager would then look for the staff member who can programme in SQL and the project will be easy. I used to teach creating the PBS this way because it made life easier for students. They could see what technical deliverables were needed. It's also the approach recommended by the British Computer Society.[1] If the BCS recommends such an approach it must therefore be a good way to go about the business of designing a PBS. Yet, all along, I felt something wasn't quite right. Why? Pretty much every PBS ended up looking the same – whatever the project characteristics. Give or take one or two different tools to use or products to produce, every product breakdown was identical. Useful for consistency in kicking off a project but are all projects the same? No, not really. Most have a good degree of variety. This made me think that there was something obvious that I was missing. What was it? The focus I had been working on was what developers need to produce, but not on what the product needs to do.

What was missing was the actual requirements themselves. Should we not focus on the features of the product we are going to build, all from the point of view of the user? No, actually. We need to broaden our perspective to also include the work done by developers that can help deliver those front-end requirements for the user. We need to take a vertical slice approach for the product's major features. This is like feature-driven development (FDD). Kanban fits well with this approach as do most project management approaches if used well or tailored to FDD.

We cannot fully understand what's in the vertical slice without a better understanding of the requirements and the structures or patterns of types of features the overall product will have. This is where we need to turn to problem frames to help us do this identification.

The last entry in Table 7.1 mentions 'product descriptions.' I personally avoid these unless there is something really vital to know about a specific thing being built or needed. Such things could be industry

Table 7.1 Relating Problem Frames and Product Breakdown Structure

Problem Frame Element	Product Breakdown Structure	Explanation
Domain of interest	Product and sub-product	The domain of interest is naturally a product. For example, if the domain is a satellite navigation screen, then it becomes a product or several sub-products that make up that screen. People do not count here but products could technically be 'trained users.'
Machine	Product section	The machine domain is the computer to be programmed but we cannot necessarily view it as the total product. We could look at a view of the final product such as in the example of the Google Translate multiframe problem where we have a Workpieces frame, a Transformation Frame and an Information Display frame.
Design domain	Product	An example would be a design domain 'Input Translation' from the Google Translate problem frame. Below this could be the complete sub-product breakdown structure. This can be seen as an example below.
Shared phenomena	N/A	N/A

(Continued)

Table 7.1 (Continued) Relating Problem Frames and Product Breakdown Structure

Problem Frame Element	Product Breakdown Structure	Explanation
Connection between domains and shared phenomena	N/A	N/A
Requirements, specification	Main products	Requirements are the main drivers for product breakdown structures. Specification isn't necessary but where we do need to define key sub-products such as certain elements of design – an entity relationship diagram – we can do so. Requirements should be sufficient but it may need specification to be more precise. This is where product descriptions may be of value.

standard certifiable quality for certain products. A product description provides a place to document this. Main products are those that form the second highest layer of the product breakdown. You can see examples below. Design domains and domains of interest can also be these main products or can be lower sub-products. The decision on what they could be is entirely subjective.

There are two entries in the table that have no discernible association and that's fine. If everything was isomorphic with everything else, then everything would basically be the same. We could have decided that 'connections between domains' in problem frames means the same as the branches on the product breakdown decomposition tree. But that's a stretch even at best. 'Shared phenomena' are data, triggers and states shared between domains or a domain and machine in problem frames. There is little to justify how this could be used in a product breakdown. Shared phenomena are probably best suited in product descriptions if they need to be represented here in the product breakdown. I have no wish to belittle data because it is vital to product and business success.

Example Product Breakdown Structure (PBS)

Figure 7.1 presents a part of the PBS for Google Translate. The PBS looks like a tree structure. What each leaf on the branches of the tree depicts are key elements of the product that need to be created. Note that this PBS is inspired by the problem frame in Chapter 3. The domains identified in the problem frame are useful in guiding the upper levels of the PBS. To get to the lower levels of the PBS from the problem frame, we need to think more about the requirements. A problem frame gives you the structure of the system to be built but not much more than that until you start to examine the requirements within the requirements oval. We have done this in the chapter on problem frames and here we can see its influence in understanding some of the products we need to create. Taken together these products not only create the actual software application but also the wider project. The reason being we are also concerned with the documentation we now need to create as part of the project. More on this later but for now let's discuss Figure 7.1.

What we see is the 'Google Translate' product at the top of the tree. This could be viewed as the machine domain in the problem frame. Then there are a number of products in the next layer: Input Translation, Output Translation and so on. Below Input Translation there are three sub-products labelled: Language recognition, User functions and Display controls. The idea of a product is something the team needs to create to help build the final deliverable, Google Translate. It's a bit like functional decomposition but with products. I wouldn't take the PBS too deep but we do need to think about how these products are going to be created. I like to think of these products as features when we are talking about the software and as project products when talking about the project. Anything that is design or code or test related, for example, is feature focussed. Things like a schedule or contract or requirements document would be viewed as project products. These project products are not features in that they are not things users can do when they use the product. They guide the build, such as a specification, but are

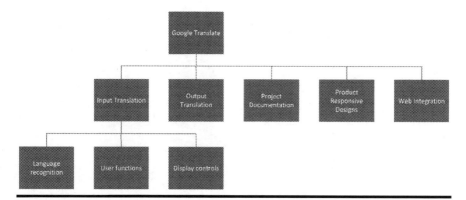

Figure 7.1 PBS for google translate: Input translation.

not the build. Problem frames are project products because they guide the actual construction.

In Figure 7.1, Language recognition is a software product that identifies the text input by the user. User functions are those functions that enable the user to edit or manipulate the text to be translated. Display controls are automatic built-in functions – that the user cannot select – to ensure that the text input by the user is actually text and not an image, for instance. The display controls also ensure the visual display on the screen is appropriate. If the user enters 20 lines of text and the interface is designed to only show a maximum of 15 lines as normal function, then the display box should expand to keep all the text visible to the user. We could decompose these lower-level products further to consider design deliverables such as object models or a database.

Let's look at another example, the Output Translation, shown in Figure 7.2.

The third layer is very similar to the Input Translation example above. One change is Translation rules. These are the Sentence restructure guide, Grammar rule check and Idiom check. The latter makes sure there are no colloquialisms in the text to be translated that may make a literal translation confused. The Sentence restructure makes sure the translation follows the new language structure as closely as possible. The Grammar rule check ensures that the translated words conform as closely as possible to the grammar of the new language – tense, article, pronouns, naming conventions and so on. There is room for significant variation in your answers. I've decided to address the rules as per the

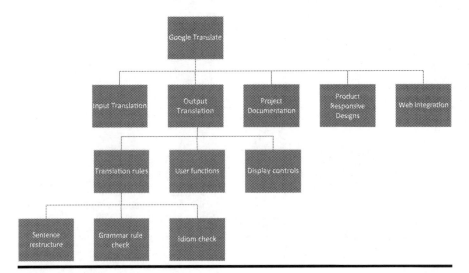

Figure 7.2 PBS output translation.

Translation rules. These rules are the requirement for successful translation. The User functions are very similar to before but also open the opportunity for the user to provide feedback on the translation. The user may be able to identify inaccuracies with the translation and can inform the Google Translate team of this. The result could be a change in the Translation rules. The Display controls product is similar again but must ensure the language is displayed correctly on the screen. If the user translates from English to Chinese, the Display control needs to ensure the correct character set is displayed, for instance.

The purpose of the PBS has traditionally been to inform the project manager of what is needed to build the product early enough in the project to create a Gantt chart, estimation durations and allocate staff. One thing that is striking is that the order of creating the PBS naturally fits in the order in which a product is built. It hardly needs saying that this is so. However, one of the tenets of the PBS 'theory' is that it does not officially present an order to development. Yet, logically, or sequentially, when thinking about waterfall-oriented projects, there is always a linear progression. So why presume that a PBS does not? I think it is to avoid placing too much pressure on the manager, initially. Focus on the products first. Order is secondary. What are we to think? For me, and I would suggest for you: assume that the PBS can represent the order of development. We have the list above already, in the normal order, so why not? I suppose it is because the PBS does not explicitly show order via one item pointing to another – creating a dependency chain – that we pretend there is no order to it.

Officially, the PBS does not impose rules for chronologically reading the diagram, and hence in its creation. Common sense, though, suggests we read the diagram top-down and left-to-right. That's how we read documents. So, I tend to put the key features on the left and as we scroll right, the lesser products appear. The idea of hierarchy in the PBS is that if everything below the top node or leaf (Google Translate in our example) is created correctly, then the project will succeed. Accordingly, if everything linked below Input Translation is built correctly, the assumption is that when combined, these leaves will make up the Input Translation.

I actually don't agree with this assumption because it presumes that the glue which binds the various elements of a project is in place automatically. By glue, I mean running regression tests, fixing bugs in an organised way and ensuring that the right product deliverables that need to talk can talk. This sweeping up work is time-consuming and traditional projects run a regular risk of forgetting about it. Indeed, agile projects probably don't allocate enough work to these tasks either. But when implementing a release management approach, they are more likely to become aware of such issues sooner.

PRODUCT BREAKDOWN STRUCTURE EXERCISE 1

You've now just read about the PBS for Google Translate and seen an example of it. Complete the following part of the Google Translate product breakdown structure:

1. Project Documentation

As ever, an example answer can be found in the Solutions Appendix 1 at the end of the book.

Note that the node Product Responsive Designs refers to the different device designs you may have to consider when accessing the app. Do you need to view Google Translate on a mobile phone or a tablet as well as on a larger computer screen from a laptop or desktop? Would the layout differ for the mobile phone view? The Web Integration node refers to how the tool may be embedded into a web screen, where it might be positioned at the top of a search engine, for instance, if the search is for a translator. This is a much more technical part of the development but a most important one.

A brief product description example:

- Product name: Grammar Rule check
- Description: The purpose of the grammar rule check is to ensure the inputted text can be translated effectively and accurately into the output language.
- Technical aspect: confirm rules documented in the Transformation problem frame to ensure the inputted language is most appropriately translated.
- Standards: coding standard as usual, Web app visualisation standards as usual
- Quality check: unit, integration, regression testing deployed. 100 per cent pass rate?

Work or Product? Breakdown Structure

There is another type of breakdown structure that relates to 'work items.' A work item links well with Kanban. A work item could be a chunk of development work that implements a requirement or user story vertically sliced from the front end all the way through to the back end, including testing, integration and, in theory, live deployment. In practice, the work item would most likely go into a production suite ready to be released at the next release cycle. The release would include many work items and ideally combine to deliver a significantly useful large slice of functionality. Releases can be every month, every two months or every three months. One project I worked on had major releases every six months which included new functionality, and minor releases every other six months mostly for fixes, patches and minor new functions. The annual release cycle: (1) big release, (2) fixes, (3) big release and (4) fixes. You might think fixes implied too many bugs and poor development. In one example, it really did but if you've noticed the continual updates you get on your computer and devices, most of these are fixes, amendments and minor changes to existing functionality.

Kanban operates on work items that are broken down into tasks through a specification step on the board. More on this later. For now, a work breakdown structure is effectively a one-stop shop for describing the product to be designed or built plus the way in which this needs to be down. A PBS is slightly cleaner in that it has only one focus – the products needed to be designed and built but with no indication of what work is needed to make the product.

This may appear to be splitting hairs and indeed when we get to Kanban we could be doing exactly that. As I have stated earlier, the normal process of traditional project management is to follow a prescriptive – and dependency driven – path (see Figure 7.3).

The traditional process of management starts with the PBS and continues all the way through to the Gantt chart. Each step is dependent

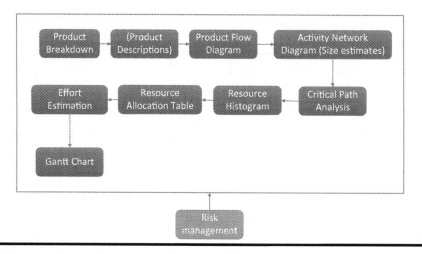

Figure 7.3 Dependency network.

upon the previous one being successful. If your size estimates are way out for tasks, then the critical path would be wrong. Resources would be deployed inaccurately as a consequence, effort estimates would be way off and the Gantt Chart would be wrong. You would be led down the garden path, as it were. All of the traditional techniques are subject to risk management. Well, not quite the techniques but project management is not really complete unless some risk analysis, mitigation and management occurs, too. The worst way to address risk management is to wave your hands and blame everyone else for a project going wrong. Better to break risks into two types: within and outside of the project.

A Note on Risk Management

'Within' project risk management is much more traditional and indeed is deployed on agile projects. The project manager focusses on what could go wrong with personnel, with budgets, with features and functions of the product and looks to mitigate against high risk 'showstoppers' that could entirely derail the project. This is perfectly good and appropriate risk management. I won't go into detail here on this topic as it is the subject of many books outside the scope of this particular one.

Where traditional risk management tends to stumble is handling of risks outside of the project. Agile leaves this risk management to the business to solve. It is outside the scope of the product being built so those working on the project can do nothing about these risks. This is the simple view. Traditional project managers even call risks outside of the boundary of the project an act of God. These managers wave their hands in the air and say there's nothing they can do. In a way, there is nothing they could have done.

Business does not look at risk management in the same way as project managers on software projects. To quote a former colleague who worked for a media mogul in Australia, when presenting the media boss with a business plan for a new venture, the mogul replied [paraphrasing]:

'Just tell me whether the innies are bigger than the outties. If they are, I'll do it.' – translated, this reads, if it looks like the venture could bring in more money that the expenditure estimated to do it, then this is risk worth taking. Business does not worry too much about minor issues when it comes to risk. After all, the nature of business is all about risk. Businesses change direction from time to time. But they do not change too much because the risk is too great. The concept of agile organisations is a bit of a misunderstanding. Businesses do need to be 'flexible' enough to deal with changes in regulation and the market place. We've seen in the corona crisis that some businesses have managed to adapt their manufacturing to keep in business in producing medical equipment. Some companies have not been able to do this and they have failed. But the corona crisis has been something extraordinary in terms of business, not something that could have been war-gamed by those businesses who went out of business. This has nothing to do with agile business at all. The whole concept of being able to change the way your business operates by deploying a Scrum approach to everything is the same pitfall that the early proponents of object-oriented analysis made, claiming that with the right coloured tint to one's glasses, you could view everything in terms of programmable objects. Life is not 'pigeonholeable' in this way because everything is connected and life throws us a curveball (baseball parlance) or googlie (cricket parlance) from time to time to keep us on our toes. These are the tests in life we need to deal with in the right way. The same happens to business. Agile companies might be able to change how they function to some extent but not completely because companies have cultures and cultures are hard to change.[2] It takes enormous effort. The Brexit chaos that the United Kingdom face at the point of leaving the EU is doubly confounding for business. The level of risk they face is massive. Doing all this in the middle of the corona chaos is ramping up the risk enormously.

Why am I writing about this in a book on requirements management and project management? All of the above have massive impact on all the projects on the go and those planned. If we put aside the massive dark shroud of uncertainty drowning most businesses right now, there are a number of core technical changes needed on IT products to deal with the new regulations on supply chain, procurement, on taxes, finances, personnel and employment law, security, value chain, customer relations... and just about everything else.

Business risk has a very big impact on projects. It is really vital that project managers working on IT projects are engaged with the business on addressing what are ostensibly labelled business risks. There is no line in the sand between IT and business any more. If you end up working as a project manager, don't ignore what the business is doing. Why does this book start with business concept models? Because business is the driver for technology. No IT business ever built a product without the opinion that everyone on the planet needs it. Very few companies end up with almost everyone using their products. Google, Facebook, Apple, Microsoft, Amazon are a few that have reached this level. Their project managers would not have lasted long if they ignored the business they were working in.

That's it for the PBS – and everything else that ended up in this chapter! It's time to move on to the Gantt chart, which we can read about next.

Notes

1 Bob Hughes (Ed), *Project-Management for IT-Related Projects*, Third Edition, British Computer Society 2019. Bob and I were office mates at the University of Brighton for about six years. Bob wrote the best book on traditional project management and put me straight on what I thought I knew about the subject. An excellent example of a product breakdown structure is found on page 36 of this edition of Bob's book.
2 An excellent book on the practicalities on bringing about cultural change for almost magical business transformation is Steven Bleistein's *Rapid Organisational Change*, published by Wiley (2018). Steve, a very successful businessman, wrote the book from his experiences of working in many countries: the US, France, Australia (where we co-owned a management consulting business) and in Japan where he now lives.

Chapter 8

Gantt Chart

The traditional Gantt chart is the culmination of a long process – some of which is described in the previous chapter. I don't wish to go through every single step because this is too much information for you and too much trouble in many projects to have to work through. Transitioning from a product breakdown structure (PBS) is good enough.

The British Computer Society (BCS) has an excellent introduction to project management which acts as the textbook for foundational project management for IT projects.[1] I like this book a lot. What's interesting about it is there is not that much energy in promoting how to construct project management tools. Far more time is given to estimation, project control and risk. Why? Because traditional projects don't work very well. They have a history of going wrong. As such, more effort goes into figuring out how to steer them more accurately to conclusion that recognising that the underlying tools used are not entirely fit for purpose. This may be considered sacrilege to write, given that the last chapter was all about traditional management and the PBS, and this chapter is also about traditional project management's top weapon, the Gantt chart. Before you think something is amiss, I would like to point out that my take on Gantt charts is not the same as the BCS version. It is almost the same but my focus is on planning requirements so they can be built into the product customers want. This is significantly different to that presented in a number of textbooks on traditional project management. If you look at the aforementioned BCS textbook, the Gantt

DOI: 10.1201/9781003168119-8

chart is shown three times in various stages of a project. What is listed as tasks on the Gantt chart are the things staff do:

A. Allocate Room
B. Recruit Staff
C. Analyse Business Processes
D. Install Infrastructure
E. Design Interface
F. Draft Acceptance Test Cases
G. Write Software
H. Devise Usability Tests
I. Carry Out Usability Tests
J. Carry Out Acceptance Tests

(p.50 in B. Hughes (ed) 2019)

This is a really useful list of tasks to perform on the project. Certainly, part of a project is to make sure there are facilities and staff to do the work (A, B in list). I most certainly concur with C Analyse Business Processes. The early part this book is all about understanding the business view (Chapter 1) and processes (Chapter 2). Then we get into the software-system development work. What infrastructure needs to be installed? Was there any architectural task listed? I am not convinced that diving into step D without having done any architectural work is a good idea. Step E is Design Interface. But for what? I know the example is from a basic, yet officially sanctioned BCS book but it is not alone – many books present a similar list. I will present one below to exaggerate this point but also elaborate on what I mean. Steps F, H, I and J are all about testing. I agree with these steps; they are vital. We finally get to the BIG step, G, Write Software. What software exactly? What are we writing? In the example, this core task is allocated seven weeks of effort. But what is being written? Where are the requirements? Below is a Gantt chart similar to the one described above I created to illustrate this type of Gantt chart approach.

This particular Gantt chart is targeted at individual computer projects that students undertake in their final year (Figure 8.1). Hence, some of the entries such as 'write research aims' and 'print 2 copies.' The similarity to the above BCS example is close. Neither is actually discussing what the product does. Both discuss tools or skills or actions deployed to *create* the product but not what the product *is*. We can accept that both the above examples are meant to be generic in intent. But this is misleading. If that were the goal, then all Gantt charts would have the same list of tasks to perform. I taught the likes

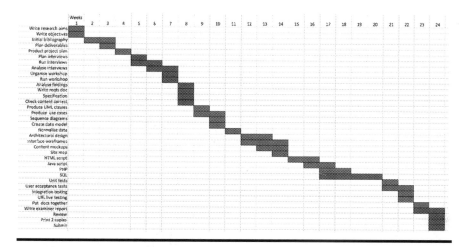

Figure 8.1 Tool list Gantt chart. This figure is taken from: K. Cox (2017), *Managing Your Individual Computing Project: An Agile Approach for Students and Supervisors* -- 2nd Edition, CreateSpace Publishing, ISBN: 978-1542778114.

of the above for some years until it dawned on me that there ought to be a clearer way to do things. If I were working from this plan, I would need to know what software to write, what SQL to code and what on earth the requirements are so I can run a project to meet them. I think this is a point where project management can become rather nebulous for students if all we do in planning is to list all the tools and techniques students learn in their degree. It appears the BCS is not too far off this mark, either. Please don't misunderstand me (which is also the title of an excellent book on team personality type!), I still think there is some value in pointing out – to students only – that they have a lot of tools to call upon in creating their product. However, this is not enough.

A more realistic Gantt chart that takes into account the Fizzit requirements is described in Figure 8.2. What stands out immediately is the inclusion of the requirements. What's missing – by design – is reference to specific tools or techniques needed to create the product. Why is this? Let's begin with the latter point first. Why not include all the different techniques and tools to create the Gantt chart? First, this is a higher-level view Gantt and we will get to breakdowns later. So why list the requirements? It makes it clear what product is being built. This makes it easier for developers to know what to build. It makes it clearer for management to pinpoint how the project is progressing by knowing what specifically is currently being worked on.

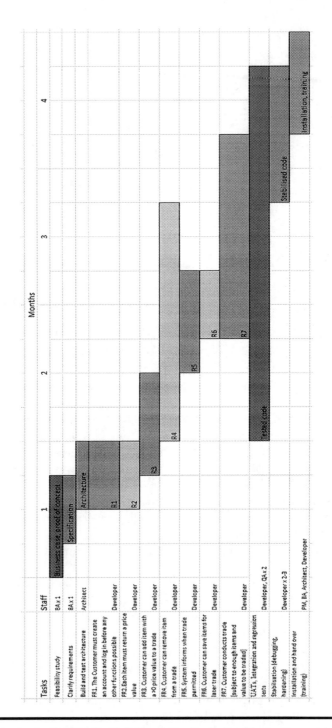

Figure 8.2 Basic ('LEGO Duplo') Fizzit Gantt chart with requirements.

As you can see in the figure, there are a number of tasks listed. These are:

Feasibility study. The goal of this task is to identify if the product idea is possible to develop given the current state of the IT department with regards to staffing, to equipment, to technical ability, to business need, to priority and to finances available. What might be the anticipated return on investment that would be the catalyst for the project to commence? The feasibility study is conducted by a business analyst and the output of this work would be a Business Case document justifying the need for the product. The business analyst would need to utilise the business concept model (Chapter 1), business process analysis (Chapter 2) and so on to convince senior management to fund the project. In some markets, such as finance, often a ball-park 20 per cent of the anticipated project cost is made available to the development team to conduct such a feasibility study. The wise manager would invest much of that money into producing a prototype of the anticipated final product. The purpose of which would be to really assess if it were worth continuing on with the main product development. Such a prototype, or proof of concept, makes or breaks the rest of the project.

Clarify requirements. This task has to be carefully managed. There is a truth in the expression 'analysis paralysis'. If we over-analyse a project, we will never get on with making the product. The issue that the agile community rebelled against the most is the misunderstanding that every requirement must be specified. This takes an enormous effort and many is the project that was smashed onto rocks in the storm of analysis paralysis. Just enough requirements specification is the realisation of Alan M. Davis.[2] He realised that you only really ever need to do enough requirements work as needed to get on with building the product. The same holds true here. The requirements tables presented earlier are really just enough to get our work done. The keyword of this task is 'clarify'. It's important to remember this point. We need to clarify that which could still be confusing. You may suspect missing elements in the requirements or you may think there are superfluous line items here. Either way, it is the role of the business analyst to do the work of clarification and documentation of outcomes.

Build and Test Architecture. This work should be conducted by a system architect and by an enterprise architect. The former focusses on the technical set-up for production of the product as well as the technical structure of the product itself. An enterprise architect would look at the wider business implications on how the organisation manages its software. Here's where the business concept model and business process models can help guide you. More technically, you might use UML component and deployment diagrams. You might look at the physical architecture of the system-to-be as well as the logical view of it. A problem frame diagram could be useful here, too. The output should be a solid architecture on which the application hangs or sits comfortably. This would typically already be in place but you will need the architect to tell you how and where this would work.

Functional Requirements FR1-7. If you recall the initial example in this chapter taken from the BCS training book, this part corresponds to the single line entry: 'write software'. We've included a line item for every major requirement. Can it really be sensible to have only one line for programming? I know it makes our plan look a lot longer but it is really important when dealing with resources to know what specifically everyone is working on. The output is working code and the staff are developers. We would need to also address quality requirements such as reliability, capacity, robustness, speed and there are security and privacy requirements, also. A development project would need to include these aspects from the word go. We don't plan explicitly for them here but performance requirements are addressed in the requirements table.

User Acceptance Tests, Integration and Regression Tests. Like the BCS example above, we impose a lot of testing on the product. This testing regime commences after the architecture and requirements 1 and 2 are completed. The testing runs until the project is nearly complete. Staff are developers and quality assurance (testing). The output of tested code should not imply that someone is working all by him or herself 100 per cent of the time on testing. One of the main complaints about the waterfall software lifecycle is that when schedules become stretched, in order to make the deadline, some key project tasks may be reduced. Testing is one thing that should never be made a secondary requirement.

Stabilisation (debugging, hardening). This task is something students will unlikely get to deal with at university. Yet it is a core part of traditional project management and indeed software development. Tested code does not mean there are no bugs that need fixing. There are always bugs in a system. A key purpose of stabilisation is to ensure the product works well enough before it gets too far out to sea. I recall working on one project where a software release had caused massive problems for the company and its clients. Yet, when talking with the QA team, they assured their employer that the number of bugs in the release was in line with other releases. They did not feel culpable. In other words, they felt it is normal to release buggy software and that this is somehow the norm. It may well be, but on this specific project, that normal quota of bugs released nearly brought the house down.

Installation and handover (training). Once the product is built, tested and approved we need to make sure the people who ordered it get it, that it works on their environment and that they know what to do with it. You may set aside whole days or even weeks to train staff in using the software. The Project Manager takes an active role in ensuring good handover. We would also ask the Architect and development team to engage in any training and installation work required. Why? Because they should be proud of their product and have a desire to encourage end users to accept it.

I've labelled Figure 8.2 'LEGO Duplo'. Why is this? For one, it looks a bit like LEGO (if you are reading this in colour). I first mentioned Duplo LEGO Gantt charts for individual student computing projects in my book *Managing Your Individual Computing Project*. The reason for this nomenclature is because in the world of LEGO, Duplo is the large version of building blocks and targeted at younger children. Models made in Duplo are simpler than the standard LEGO. The same is said for the Gantt chart in Figure 8.2. The question we need to ask is if this block Gantt chart is good enough? The answer is always: it depends. Most of the core things that need to be done are listed, after all. All that being said, there still needs, for most projects, more focus. What exactly needs to be done for requirement 1? Or requirement 5? Experienced developers can work from the requirement itself but they do need to clarify with colleagues what the tricky or time-consuming elements of the requirement will be. As such, we need to look more closely at the requirements or features of the product.

Feature-Driven Development (FDD)

Is not only agile! Almost everywhere you look, you will see FDD listed with agile modelling.[3] This is correct but I think we can also adopt an FDD approach in our planning here. It seems to me that FDD fits well with a PBS the way they are described in the previous chapter. We are, after all, dividing the product up according to its main features. These we could loosely describe as the core requirements – not the other aspects such as project documentation. I fully buy into the idea that a design for a screen is as much part of the screen's development as its code because design is a part of the software development lifecycle. When we get to Kanban, you will see that FDD is fundamental though we might actually here and now rename FDD to TDD: task-driven development.

Task-Driven Development?

As you will see in the next chapter, Kanban operates with tasks. I argue here that traditional project management of development work also operates with tasks. But there is a limit and that is only those tasks pertaining to actual development work can be considered as part of task-driven development. Looking at Figure 8.1, we see a long list of tools to be deployed on a project that are used to fulfill tasks. We do not know, however, for what requirement(s) they are being used. We are effectively blindly developing a product. Figure 8.2 takes us out of the paradigm of listing all the skill sets we need to addressing the requirements more appropriately. What skills are to be deployed we leave to the developers, working in accord with their line manager and project manager. However, we do not know what designs or tools requirements 1 or 2 or the architecture need to be completed. Here we can turn to the PBS to see the organisation of potential products.

The PBS shown in Appendix 2 is part of the model for the Fizzit case and breaks the Fizzit system into five main areas or modules: architecture, conducting a trade, drop-off location, quality assurance check, customer payment. These last four mirror the requirements groupings set out in Appendix 2 and are the main modules of the Fizzit software, relating to the business process as well as providing context.

Under 'Conducting a Trade' there are four sub-products. Each refers to at least one requirement listed in Appendix 2. But rather than copying the requirement out, we again group into like-minded areas. For instance, there are four separate requirements that relate to the customer trade in this module: requirements 3, 4, 5 and 7. Rather than listing them separately, we can create a generic product called Trade Screen Function.

Under 'FR1. Account/login', there are three potential sub-products: (i) 'screen design', which refers to any aspects of the login and account creation we need to consider in detail; (ii) 'Database tables' refers to the management of the database in creating new records for the new client, for instance; and, (iii) we need to address 'Security and Privacy controls' to ensure the client data is kept secure. I've labelled the PBS figure as 'partial' because it is not complete. Much more space would be needed to show an end-to-end complete model. In Appendix 2, I have included a wider PBS to address all the requirements for Conduct a Trade. I have also removed a product that you see in Figure 8.3, namely the 'Screen Design' sub-product that hangs from the FR1 requirement. The reason being that it does not take a massive effort to design a login screen. There's a bit more to it than that and I do include this product here in this chapter for reasons of clarity. However, from a wider viewpoint, it may not be necessary to document.

Creating the Gantt Chart

How do we include the sub-products into a Gantt chart? That's relatively straightforward to do though it does take up more space on the chart itself. We don't include the products so much as the tasks we need to undertake to create those so-called sub-products. If we take our encouragement from a task-driven development, which is a more concrete feature-driven development, then it is a straightforward endeavour to create the Gantt chart, even if time-consuming. We need the PBS to guide us in doing so. As explained earlier, the PBS is created by an examination of the requirements. Thus, what is included in the Gantt chart is a task or set of tasks that help make the product or sub-product as described in the PBS.

If we look at the following snippet of a Gantt chart for the Fizzit project (Figure 8.3), we can see that there are functional requirements listed, FR2 and FR3. These directly refer to the requirements. Below each requirement, indented, are three tasks needed to help build the requirement. For FR2, this is FR2.1, FR2.2 and FR2.3. This is a correct way to label the subtasks and these relate directly to the sub-products in the PBS (see Appendix 2).

Note that for FR3, the tasks have not been labelled in the same way because our manager forgot to include the labels. This oversight can cause problems. It is important to label all tasks appropriately to maintain traceability – and hence understanding – between the models. You can also see that some of the naming of the tasks is somewhat bland for FR3. Screen designs need to be assessed for usability. This is a vital aspect of all systems, if the goal is to have them used. To label 'Usability screen design' might be a bit naïve but in reality it is informing the design team that usability has to be the focus of attention. 'Secure function' is a rather vague description. What does it mean? It is not very well written but in essence it means the requirement FR3 must be secure. Extra security – because the user accesses a trade account which in turn is potentially linked to bank account details – must be adopted in its implementation. 'Database tables' is again a little bland and should be

◢ FR2.Each item must return a price value	10 days	Mon 25/01/2 Fri 05/02/21 5	
FR2.1. Screen designs	2 days	Mon 25/01/2: Tue 26/01/21	
FR2.2 ISBN Database tables	5 days	Mon 25/01/2: Fri 29/01/21	
FR2.3 Price value update engine	10 days	Mon 25/01/2: Fri 05/02/21	
◢ FR3. Customer can add item with a >0 price value to a trade	5 days?	Mon 01/02/21 Fri 05/02/21	
Usability screen designs	2 days	Mon 01/02/2 Tue 02/02/2:	
Secure function	5 days	Mon 01/02/: Fri 05/02/21	
Database tables	4 days	Mon 01/02/: Thu 04/02/2:	

Figure 8.3 Gantt chart snippet. All Microsoft Project screen images in this book are used with permission from Microsoft.

more precisely worded to refer to the creation and testing of any database modification that is needed so the requirement can function as it is intended. Even when a Gantt chart is produced, it can still be difficult to follow or interpret. Being as precise but succinct as you can helps tremendously.

Some students break tasks into something like the following:

FR1. ... whatever it is...
Gather requirements
Design screens
Programme
Test code

I can understand why they do this. There is some consistency in task allocation and number, which in turn leads to a supposedly more consistent effort estimate or duration calculation. In principle, this is the right approach but there are some issues with it, though. For instance, the header, FR1 and the requirement description makes the first task, Gather requirements, redundant. 'Design screens' is fine if it is something that needs serious consideration. I use it in my example above. 'Programme' or 'Code' is an important task to be done, and needs to be documented in a Gantt chart so that the right resource can be allocated. But code what? More description will be needed. I might not even explicitly mention 'code' as is but would focus on a very specific element, such as 'ISBN database tables' or to task-ify it, 'import, tailor and test ISBN database tables.' For succinctness, we refer to 'ISBN database tables' only. It is the manager's responsibility to find out how work is progressing on this important facet. What modifications were needed to tailor the ISBN database to our needs and is that work done? Has it been appropriately tested, who is doing the work and when will it be completed? We could reuse this argument for each task listed, including 'design screens' which could include design, programming and testing.

GANTT CHART EXERCISE 1

Complete the Fizzit Gantt chart for Functional Requirement 1:

FR1. The Customer must create an account and log in before any other functions possible.

As ever, an example answer can be found in the Solutions Appendix 1.

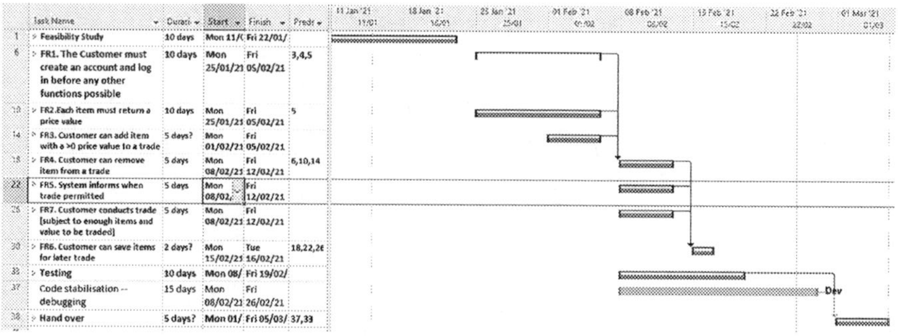

Figure 8.4 Overall Gantt chart.

The 'Test code' task is important to include so that unit tests are conducted. But is this testing not included already within for example the 'ISBN database tables'? The completed product or sub-product would at some point have to be integrated into the existing system and then further tests such as regression tests will have to be conducted. Such testing traditionally takes place later in the project.

You can create a general Gantt chart that can give you a bigger picture view. Figure 8.4 presents an example from our case study.

This is a high-level view similar to the example in Figure 8.2. I like this birds-eye view because we can see the whole project plan. There is almost no detail other than the main requirements and the order in which they should be built. As we will see in the following chapter on Kanban, having an overview Gantt chart can be a good idea. We can add more detail. The following Figure 8.5 shows a part Figure 8.4 expanded.

Traditional planning likes to include milestones. A milestone indicates when a specified amount of work or collection of functions should be completed. The idea would be to include these into the first Gantt chart and to deliver these on schedule. I don't include milestones normally because I focus on the requirements anyway. However, this is dependent upon the contractual agreement with your client. If the contract states there will be staged deliveries of groups of requirements, each of which results in payment for that amount of completed work, then you could add a milestone to the Gantt chart. Or keep it in the contract. Either way, you would group the work to address these phased deliverables.

Resources are allocated onto the Gantt chart. You could include the actual names of people. This would make a lot of sense when you know everyone on the team. I don't think that helps us here for the sake of explanation. So being very generic, I have used job roles instead as can be seen in Figure 8.5. I've kept roles very simple. Here, you can see

Task Name	Duration	Start	Finish	Pred	Resource Names
FR1.1. Screen designs	2 days	Mon 25/01/2:	Tue 26/01/21		UXD
FR1.2. Database Tables	4 days	Wed 27/01/2:	Mon 05/02/2: 7		DBA
FR1.5. Security and privacy controls	4 days	Tue 02/02/21	Fri 05/02/21 8		Dev
FR2.Each item must return a price value	10 days	Mon 25/01/2:	Fri 05/02/21 5		
FR2.1. Screen designs	2 days	Mon 25/01/2:	Tue 26/01/21		UXD
FR2.2. SSN Database tables	5 days	Mon 25/01/2:	Fri 29/01/21		DBA
FR2.3 Price value update engine	10 days	Mon 25/01/2:	Fri 05/02/21		Dev
FR3. Customer can add item with a >0 price value to a trade	5 days?	Mon 01/02/21	Fri 05/02/21		
FR3.1. Usability screen designs	2 days	Mon 01/02/2:	Tue 02/02/2:		UXD
FR3.2. Secure function	5 days	Mon 01/02/2:	Fri 05/02/21		Dev
FR3.3. Database tables	4 days	Mon 01/02/2:	Thu 04/02/2:		DBA
FR4. Customer can remove item from a trade	5 days	Mon 08/02/2:	Fri 12/02/21 6,10,14		
FR4.1. Usability screen designs	2 days	Mon 08/02/2:	Tue 09/02/2:		UXD
FR4.2. Secure function	5 days	Mon 08/02/2:	Fri 12/02/21		Dev
FR4.3. Database tables	4 days	Mon 08/02/2:	Thu 11/02/2:		DBA
FR5. System informs when trade permitted	5 days	Mon 08/02/2:	Fri 12/02/21		
FR5.1. Usability screen designs	2 days	Mon 08/02/2:	Tue 09/02/2:		UXD
FR5.2. Secure function	5 days	Mon 08/02/2:	Fri 12/02/21		Dev
FR5.3. Database tables	4 days	Mon 08/02/2:	Thu 11/02/2:		DBA
FR7. Customer conducts trade (subject to enough items and value to be traded)	5 days	Mon 08/02/21			
FR7.1. Usability screen designs	2 days	Mon 08/02/2:	Tue 09/02/2:		UXD
FR7.2. Secure function	5 days	Mon 08/02/2:	Fri 12/02/21		Dev
FR7.3. Database tables	4 days	Mon 08/02/2:	Thu 11/02/2:		DBA
FR6. Customer can save items for later trade	2 days?	Mon 15/02/2:	Tue 16/02/21 18,22,26		
FR6.1. Screen designs (usability)	1 day	Mon 15/02/2:	Mon 15/02/2:		UXD,Dev
FR6.2. Database tables	2 days	Mon 15/02/2:	Tue 16/02/2:		DBA
Testing	10 days	Mon 08/02/2:	Fri 19/02/21		QA,Dev,T

Figure 8.5 Expanded Gantt chart. A larger portion of the Gantt chart for Fizzit can be found in Appendix 2.

there are three roles: DBA, Dev and UXD. DBA is a database administrator or database developer. Dev is a programmer or developer. UXD is a user experience designer or HCI expert. The figure does not explicitly state the number of staff. My view on this project is that one UXD and DBA are enough for the whole project. One Dev may also be enough. Requirements FR4, FR5 and FR7 are done in parallel and it could be possible for the user experience designer to design all the screens, for the database specialist to design and code the database and for the developer to connect the front and back end, and get it working well. In the case of a project you might undertake at university in groups, you need to know the job roles are filled and rather than keeping it generic, you would add your personal name to the task or tasks you need to do.

I urge you to take a good look at Appendix 2 which contains more of the Gantt chart presented in Figure 8.5. If you produced this Gantt chart for a project, or something equivalent, showing your prediction of how the project will go, what will be developed when and by whom, how close do you think the final project plan would look like to the original – if you had to keep it updated on a daily basis – once the project finished? I can bet not very similar at all. But you put such effort into creating it the first place and more effort in maintaining it. Was it worth it? Would a better way to use Gantt charts have made life easier, one in which you kept to a simple overall view like in Figure 8.4? But what of the nitty gritty work needed to be done, where would you document this? Personally, I would use a Kanban board for detailed development and run that development in a Kanban way. Let's take a look in the next chapter.

Notes

1 Bob Hughes (Ed), *Project-Management for IT-Related Projects*, Third Edition, British Computer Society 2019.
2 Alan M. Davis, *Just Enough Requirements Management*, Dorset House Publishing, 2005.
3 For example, http://agilemodeling.com/essays/fdd.htm. FDD was initially co-developed by Peter Coad, developer of the Coad-Yourdon OOA-D notation. I was taught this in the pre-UML days.

Chapter 9

Kanban Boards

Kanban boards are very popular in project management and are used primarily in agile development. There are degrees of complexity of usage of Kanban from the simplest set of boards: To Do, Doing, Done to more complex ones. We will go a bit beyond this simple set to provide a little more structure in our Kanban board. The last chapter described Gantt charts. We might ask ourselves if we need two project management tools. I would say not but upon inspection, aspects of the Gantt chart can be very valuable if used appropriately alongside the Kanban board.

A Gantt chart can be compared to a Kanban board:

- Both have a deadline… but work continues until it is done (although this is not always the case).
- Development tasks in a Gantt chart match those on a Kanban board.
- Features or requirements in a Gantt chart match the work items or stories in the product backlog section on a Kanban board.

A Gantt chart is different in that it calculates and presents durations for tasks or requirements on the chart whereas Kanban assumes an average duration for completing tasks (Task Completion Rate - TCR) per day. This does not mean that the average holds true every day – it is just an average. You could organise the Gantt chart in such a way as to address this task estimation. Take an average rather than rely upon estimation calculations such as function points or use case points per requirement. If we work with a standard set of tasks it will force developers to rethink how requirements are specified and broken into tasks. There will need

DOI: 10.1201/9781003168119-9

to be some uniformity. This is something not typical in traditional project management. In Kanban, the idea is in a project there will be a lot of requirements and to spend time trying to identify nuances and minute differences in effort of each component is going to take a long time. The last thing you need concern yourself with in project estimation is calculation paralysis. In a university setting, estimating project durations is really pointless because there are hard deadlines that cannot be skipped if students want to pass their assessment. Students have to do as much as possible in the time permitted to deliver the best product they can. The finer elements of management that may be needed in practice do not often come into play at university for students.

Ironically, even though hard deadlines are the norm on degree courses, Gantt and Kanban are both best suited to continuous development where the deadline, though set, can easily slip so the work can be completed to expectation. I don't think Gantt charts or Kanban are suited to hard deadlines because they both focus on delivering all the agreed requirements. Scrum, for instance, doesn't do it quite like this, sticks to a hard deadline and delivers what it can of the core/must have requirements in that timeframe. The remaining requirements are left until another project. Yet, Gantt and Kanban are, in my opinion, the two most straightforward project management approaches for students. They are visually understandable and this makes it easy to know what to do. A couple of uses and they are almost self-explanatory once the basics have been grasped. Agile tools like burndown charts are a little less easy to understand and approaches like Scrum take some understanding, too. Students will really experience agile sprints once they are out in practice. In the classroom, this is not very easy to simulate. The best 'agile' approach for a university setting as such, in my view, is Kanban for group projects.

Kanban estimation works out the time to complete a project based on current task estimates (task completion rate, task add rate and number of tasks remaining to be completed). This is very similar to most estimation approaches and that's normal. What makes the two approaches – Kanban and Gantt – more similar is the idea of working out how much faster staff need to work to deliver work tasks, if behind schedule (based upon their estimates) or in adding more staff to a project if it looks like it will overrun so as to make the deadline. Traditional project management estimation works in the same way in principle. More staff can be added even if the project looks like it is going to be late. This approach is common even though it violates Brooks's Law.[1] Kanban suggests the same thing. I am pretty confident that Brooks's Law holds in both approaches. The more people added to a project when it is late will only make it later. Why? Because new staff need time to get up to speed on the project and the only people who can get them up to speed on what has already been produced are the ones producing it. The staff already on the project need to take time out of it to educate the new staff. Lower throughput rates ensue and the new staff typically work more slowly when they join the project. This is entirely understandable if you think about it. At the start of any project, things go more slowly because it isn't always clear what needs to be done or how it should be done. It is only when a few weeks have passed on the project that staff tend to get into an optimal way of working: efficiently working with each other collaboratively. If you take this into consideration at the end of a project and add to the equation the impending deadline, pressure from clients, management and rising stress rates, then throwing new staff into the mix at that point will more likely derail the project more quickly. In practice, it is important to realise the risk of adding people late in the project. Estimates on completion dates should be worked out early enough to be able to add staff then and there – if it is estimated that the time to complete the work (based on completed task rate) looks like it is going to go significantly beyond the agreed completion date of the project. Adding staff now will allow enough time for the new member(s) of the team to work their way into the project slowly enough to be able to maintain good quality but with enough lead time to get up to speed and contribute to bringing forward the estimated time to complete.[2]

Often a project manager on a traditional project will recognise that the project is going to overrun before it happens. The project manager and team will already know they are in trouble but it is usually management above them, deciding on budget expansion and staff levels that are slow to acknowledge something has gone wrong. Projects are often accepted on budgets that are way too small to complete on schedule. I have experienced this myself with a project to build a product for my company. I managed the product development, establishing the requirements and cutting them to as minimal as I thought feasible for a minimum viable product. I worked with colleagues to identify the right development company to build the product because unfortunately and unwisely, my employer had a hiring freeze in place so we couldn't hire staff to build the product. The IT department was maxed-out already on other work with a minimal skeleton crew. We had to outsource the development. The company I hired – an excellent, small IT house – ended up having a lot of staffing issues and we had a rigid and very inflexible budget of only $100,000 Australian dollars. Our goal was to build a beta prototype to take to the Australian market, and to get enough of a business line with it for wider investment to turn the prototype into a much more battle-hardened software tool, offered as a SaaS (software as a service) product. The development company did a great job but the project was hampered by their staffing issues. All in, I ended up with six project managers to work with in the space of six months. It was an experience for me! The development company eventually got most of the product built despite staff leaving them at a rate of knots. Towards the end, the CEO of the company met with me to discuss the finances. We had zero extra budget and he was struggling to cover costs because his staff turnover delayed the project by 100 per cent. It took twice as long to make as originally scheduled. To help the CEO out, I cut a number of functions from the requirements and he managed the final development steps. These were functions I did not want to cut. He'd added all the staff he could afford and it was not enough to get the project done. Added to this, some of my features needed very unique modelling functionality, requiring the use of embedding software into my product they were unfamiliar with. My company were not going to approve more budget – well, they did an extra $1000 – so we were in a situation of the project already overrunning and about to cost the development company far more than it could afford. What can you do? Turn the screw on them? No, you have to be understanding so I eased up any pressure on them and took effectively what they had built as the final deliverable, with a bit more polishing here and there.

A lot of projects don't have such accommodating endings. In my case, I realised that neither side was going to win if I held out or they did. So, I compromised to make sure we got something and they didn't dig into their own budget. I've discussed earlier in the book that traditional projects can fail for a number of reasons, this example described being one of them. Kanban can have similar risk of overrun but a Kanban project is a little different. Much of the distinction lies on how to address dependencies.

Gantt does have a dependency concern that agile development tries to avoid until it is impossible to do so. The Gantt chart conveys a hard-line dependency or order in which work is done. If you look at Appendix 2, the Fizzit case study, you will see a Gantt chart where some requirements and tasks depend upon others to have completed before they commence. This creates a schedule in the Gantt chart of what work to do first, second, third and so on. We have to be very careful that the right ordering is in place. How do you determine this? We should consider prioritisation of business need as the mechanism for determining the order of implementation. This means a lot of consultation with the business team and again highlights how important it is to have a business concept model and business process models documented. The Gantt chart is also front loaded. In other words, we are predicting the order of work, the duration of the work items or tasks and the timing of this work before we have even begun. I still think Gantt charts are useful but, in all honesty, managing them through a project is tough. I really think the bigger picture they present of the project work as foreseen ahead of development makes them a really good baseline tool to use. For inexperienced developers this is a crucial advantage because they can keep coming back to the bigger Gantt picture to get an idea of how work is progressing against the broader plan. But the Gantt approach imposes a rigidity on schedules, on development and on staffing that can feel stifling.

Contrast this to the freedom of a Kanban board, where developers can pick and choose what to build. They may think there are some dependencies and thus build the product in the order suited, but also, they may choose to ignore dependencies to build what they think is the next thing to do. Kanban frees you from having to pre-schedule everything which is a strength especially on a volatile requirements list, but it is also a weakness. When you pile up all the requirements or work items or user stories and so on in the 'To Do' or 'Backlog' board, it can seem a little daunting. So much work to do. As a project continues, work may be moving slowly across the board and you may be bogged down in that work. If you look up and take a peek at the board, you can see the Backlog is still clogged up. Not much has made it right across the board, if anything. The next question you might ask is where should we already be on our project? The Kanban board does not provide an answer because it only ever tells you where you are right now. You could be miles behind schedule but the board won't point it out to you explicitly. You can guess easily enough, if almost nothing has moved across the board. But where ought you be by now? Unclear. Unless you have a Gantt chart to give you that bigger view. Projects change all the time; easy tasks suddenly become headaches and long tasks get done in a day. That's how it goes. A Gantt chart, therefore, will not be very accurate. You're guessing, anyway, when planning it out. But it will offer a ballpark estimate. And that is good enough. Before we get on to some example Kanban boards, we've reached the key point about Gantt and Kanban I wish to make.

Together, they work well. Gantt, on its own, presents a good idea overview starting point – which can be broken into tasks as shown in the Kanban board below.[3]

Before we get to this, I would like to point out the type of Kanban board that you will often see depicted as only three columns. This is the one most often cited as used in conjunction with Scrum. The board's columns are To Do, Doing, Done. This works well on simple short burst projects. It is very simple for a reason and that is to keep the amount of ongoing work – the Doing – at the minimum to avoid overload. An example is presented next.

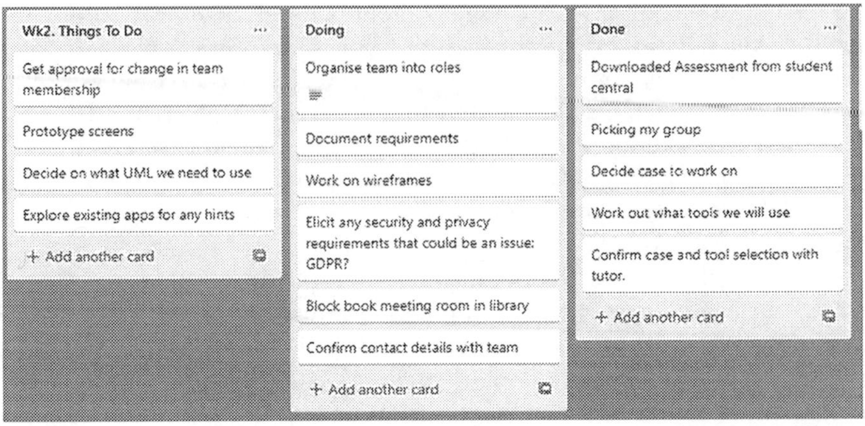

Wk2. Things To Do ⋯	Doing ⋯	Done ⋯
Get approval for change in team membership	Organise team into roles	Downloaded Assessment from student central
Prototype screens	Document requirements	Picking my group
Decide on what UML we need to use	Work on wireframes	Decide case to work on
Explore existing apps for any hints	Elicit any security and privacy requirements that could be an issue: GDPR?	Work out what tools we will use
+ Add another card	Block book meeting room in library	Confirm case and tool selection with tutor.
	Confirm contact details with team	+ Add another card
	+ Add another card	

Figure 9.1　Basic three-column Trello board.

As depicted in Figure 9.1, there are three columns. The first, labelled Wk2. Things To Do lists all the ideas for functions, products, sub-products, deliverables, documents, research and so on that you think your project will need to do. The Doing column presents all the ongoing work that is current and yet to be finished. Much of it is development work, but it can also include organisational tasks like booking meeting rooms and ensuring the team's contact details are up-to-date. The Done column lists all the tasks that have been completed and signed off. As you can see, the example shows a student group assignment set-up. Why is the first board labelled Wk2? These are the identified tasks to be done during week 2 and possibly beyond. If you are working with such a board, you can take weekly screenshots or images so you can keep a record of progress.

There is a different structure to the Kanban board that I prefer for more complex projects. It has more columns but these are subdivided. On the Trello board this is show by column placed next to column, a list of which is presented.

- ■ Backlog
- ■ Specify Active
- ■ Specify Done
- ■ Implement Active
- ■ Implement Done
- ■ Validate Active
- ■ Validate Done[4]

It's quite a bit different to the three-column board because 'Doing' in Figure 9.1 equates to Specify Active, Specify Done, Implement Active, Implement Done, Validate Active. Perhaps you can see why I prefer the longer board. See the below figures to get a better understanding. Putting all of the above end-to-end development work into 'Doing' does not always give developers enough understanding of the complexity they are facing. It also downplays Specification and Validation as minor tasks or even forgettable. For experienced developers, this is something they don't forget but for students, such a simple board structure can aid in forgetting the range of things you need to address.

What the Columns Mean

Backlog – the main features, functions, requirements we need to deliver in the product. We can also include university deliverables such as project reports and individual contributions.

Specify Active – an analyst takes one of the items in the backlog and places it into the Specify Active column. At this point, the analyst will review the backlog and decide whether any of it needs further analysis, such as the creation of a diagram like a use case. It may be the analyst will have to formally specify certain requirements if the system is critical. Once the item is assessed in this way, the output is a number of tasks.

Specify Done – this is where the analyst moves the tasks as a result of the analysis and specification work. To ensure the work is of good enough quality, certain tests must be passed called the 'Done' Rules. The rules are set at the start of the project and two of the project team – the person who did the work and a colleague familiar with the type of work – agree the work is accurate and complete. Done rules for Specify might be 'traceability clear', 'all use cases linked to requirements', 'formal specification internal validity correct'. Done rules are also found in the Implement Done column and might include for example, integration and regression tests must passed with a 100 per cent rating.

Implement Active – the developer will take a task from the Specify Done column and move it into the Implement Active column. Here the developer will work on any designs needed and will programme the task. Work items in the backlog that were broken into tasks need to be 'reassembled' here in order that when validation occurs, the customers or users are validating against their requirements as described in the backlog.

Implement Done – the work item (or the set of tasks the item consists of) is then placed into the Implement Done column provided it has passed all the Done rules for implementation.

Validate Active – this column comes into play when the project team want to sign off the work. Two team members will demonstrate the completed work item to users or customers and run through user acceptance tests. With their approval the work is signed off. If an item is not approved because, for instance, the requirement was misunderstood and some of its development did not meet expectations, the item will be returned to the Backlog with a 'Bug Fix' label, if it cannot easily be fixed during the validation session. The 'Bug Fix' item will be treated in the same way as any item in the Backlog. However, it may also be 'frozen' – not allowed to cross the board – until more clarity on it has been found by the development team in consultation with the customer. This freezing is common when requirements are misunderstood. Whenever an unclear requirement is identified, it is immediately frozen (cannot progress further across the board) until all has been clarified to the satisfaction of the developers and the customer/user.

Validate Done – all completed work, signed off by customers, clients and end users, is placed here. The completed work should have been integrated into the next release or live product and have been regression and integration tested, all tests passed 100 per cent.

The following two examples (Figures 9.2 and 9.3) show various phases of the Trello board for the Fizzit case particularly around paying the Customer and the three-strikes policy.

We can see four columns: Backlog, Specify Active, Specify Done and Implement Active in Figure 9.2. In the Backlog we have FR17 still to develop.[5] Specify Active contains FR16, which means the analyst is breaking this function into manageable chucks or tasks. Specify Done contains FR15.2 and FR15.3 plus the Done Rules to check the specification tasks are acceptable quality. This means that FR15 has already been broken into smaller tasks. Two tasks are in the Implement Active column, FR14.4 and FR15.1, meaning that these two tasks are in the

Figure 9.2 Placing resources into the board.

Figure 9.3   Through to validate done.

process of being programmed. We also added resources to the board by allocating tasks to staff. There are three showing on the board: KC, C and N. All staff are responsible for checking work meets the quality criteria established by the Done rules.

Figure 9.3 shows the columns from Implement Active through to Validate Done. We've explained Implement Active above. Implement Done shows FR14.3 has been programmed and is awaiting approval according to the Done Rules. FR14.1 is in the Validate Active column. This means FR14.1 has passed all the tests in the implementation phase. Two members of staff, KC and N, are conducting the validation. The validation is normally done with the user, user group, customer and/ or client. The process of validation is the trial of the software function within the application – it has already been integrated as part of the implementation phase. Students rarely get to validate their work with a real customer or end user, so in this circumstance, provided the Done Rules are met for the validation, we can accept the task as validated.

This is the basis for Kanban, agile-oriented development. You place an item from the Backlog into the Specify Active column, break it into tasks and work on developing or delivering whatever those tasks ask for. Eventually, all tasks end up in the Validate Active and Done columns if all goes well. The benefit of Kanban shows that you can, if you so choose, develop one work item end-to-end at a time. This is subject to your team size and is driven by priorities.

Why Do We Need So Many Columns?

Other than more easily managing complexities in development, we have to deal with throughput. One of the driving factors to Kanban is the idea of ensuring work progresses at maximum efficiency by not overloading the slowest area of development. If Implementation is an area that takes your team longer to do than Specification, piling up work into the Specify Done column would put huge pressure on the developers to rush through their work to keep up with the inflow. Consequently, we would limit the amount of work performed in Specification to enable just the right amount of work to flow into the Implementation. This is always an estimate but managing the flow ensures the team can get on with the work as efficiently as possible without feeling too pressured by workload pile-up and by not feeling they are causing a bottleneck. Traditional development often results in bottlenecks or pile-ups: All the analysis has to be done before any development work can commence. How do developers feel watching the work pile-up and up and up? Kanban takes a more sensible approach to this aspect of work life. I won't go into how to calculate throughput in this book because this is something students won't really have to deal with at university on a group development project. I would teach this estimate approach, though, in my classes!

KANBAN BOARD EXERCISE 1

Complete a Fizzit Kanban board from Specify Active to Implement Active for Functional Requirement 1:

> *FR1. The Customer must create an account and log in before any other functions possible.*
> As ever, an example answer can be found in the Solutions Appendix 1.

Notes

1 Frederick Brooks Jr (1995), Mythical Man-Month, The: Essays on Software Engineering, Anniversary Edition, Addison-Wesley.
2 Eric Brechner (2015), *Agile Project Management with Kanban*, Microsoft Press. Microsoft use Kanban to develop the X-Box.
3 Permission to present Kanban board examples created using Trello is granted by Atlassian (https://www.atlassian.com/). Trello can be found at https://trello.com/home. Atlassian is an excellent company from Australia. Their tool suite ranges from JIRA to Confluence and Kanban, and much more.
4 This structure is used by Microsoft. See: Eric Brechner (2015), *Agile Project Management with Kanban*, Microsoft Press.
5 Note that these functional requirements are taken from Appendix 2.

Chapter 10

Summary

I set out to write a guide solely to provide extra material for students in my classes. The original idea was to prepare a lot of slides that students could access to help explain aspects of different models. I never intended to put it all together in a book. But here we are and the original concept in my head for this is now something quite different. I was preoccupied with filling gaps. There were gaps where students could not get the idea that business needs IT to support it. Well, they got that but just what should a business analyst do to help link two worlds? It's not easy to do this.

I did not intend to introduce business concept models into the book but they became very important because processes don't capture business intent very well. Concept models are needed to explore what businesses intend to do. At which point, we can begin to think about how the business will make good on its intention. If you start with processes, as is often the case, the intention is missing. If you bypass business process modelling, then you run into problems of not knowing where things that flow into and out of an organisation go. Customer orders flow through a company and you need to track where they go, who they connect with, into which database they dive and what ultimately becomes of them. Business process modelling can give you this detail. If you're introducing new systems or modifying existing ones, it is a great idea to look where in the wider process those new or modified actions fit.

Connecting everything together in the book, you will have seen:

1. There is a business idea to address/business problem to solve (I prefer the former because it is much more positive though I recognise business problems often drive IT solutions). We began by looking at a business concept model, which gives us a shared understanding of the business domain.
2. From this concept model, we reviewed how our business processes are affected. We modelled processes using the business process modelling notation diagram (BPMN).
3. Abstract system architecture emerged and was represented as problem frames.
4. We needed to also document requirements and began to detail ('specify') them.
5. Use cases come into play when documenting requirements where necessary, linking them to the BPMN model and problem frames.
6. Then we moved into the world of project management and presented a product breakdown structure to begin with, showing how it could be co-developed from a problem frame diagram.
7. A Gantt chart could then be developed from the product breakdown, requirements and use cases. We introduced the idea of task-driven development, realising this is good fit with Kanban.
8. A Kanban board was used to manage the development parts of the project, driven by the Gantt chart, taking into consideration the tasks from the specification of requirements.

I hope at least some of this made sense. The odd chapter out, probably for most readers, is the one on problem frames. Even I find that they can be a bit awkward because they do not fit easily with approaches like UML. But I have a long history with problem frames and a close association. I like that they try to get you to think differently and to recognise patterns. Whether you use them, I leave to you. Where I have used them, I have had to really think about what I have been doing: grown-up software development someone once called it. Problem frames is its own methodology all by itself. The progression of problems is a way to think about how systems work with the wider world, link by link. Problem frames never caught on in the research community save for a handful of people, of which I was one. I think this is because they broke the mould of how academics should think about analysis. The main mould at the time was UML, of which I was also a fan. I include use cases in this book because I am still a fan.

Requirements and use cases can fit together but I split them into two chapters so as not to mix terminology and throw too much at you in one go. Requirements are often tabled and in this book you get to see one way of doing it. There are many ways and where you end up working will have its own unique way to table requirements. The elements of requirements specification as documented help you to see there is more to capture than simply the basic requirement itself. Use cases are used heavily in software development so knowing how to draw the diagrams and write the descriptions especially is a distinct advantage.

The second part of the book has looked at three project management tools that I find the most useful for students when they need to get a project up and running. The discussion on project management tools is very limited because students have very limited opportunities to run projects. Having to pour through bucketloads of different project management tools is simply not feasible for students driven by hard deadlines and some concern over the purpose of project planning. They have very short time scales and the deliverables are almost never rolled out beyond their module or unit they are undertaking. We don't need to introduce heavyweight management here. I could have written about risk management but students don't have to deal with it other than getting their teammates to contribute and to ensure they hit the submission deadline. Business risks are not a factor. Ironically, an unforeseen risk presented me the opportunity to write the book – the corona lockdowns. This also had a massive impact on all of my students, especially those engaging in group projects because they could not meet face-to-face with their group members. Most students managed by using the online tools available but the removal of that face-to-face, in the same room, meeting made the students' job of managing their group activities much harder. They did learn about distributed software development not by design but by circumstance! I am proud of the students' resilience in the face of such a situation. So risk became a big part of managing their group projects after all and most of the risk was about communication management. This I mentioned at the start of the book, communication misunderstandings are at the heart of business-IT misalignment.

I really only wanted to highlight the relationship between requirements and project management all the way from the business view to the technology view in this book. This is addressed to a large extent, I hope. When we are in the realm of Gantt charts and the Kanban board, students will see that it is only by decomposing the requirements into tasks that we can plan in detail.

I trust the exercises in the book have helped you get to grips with the techniques. I had to leave aspects of notation out of all the requirements and management tools described here because each tool by itself is a book. As I said, I wanted to provide just what was needed to assist in completing assignments. I hope I have done this.

One aspect of the early lifecycle I wanted to write about but simply didn't have space or time is security and privacy requirements identification and management, and how these come into play in a project, using the tools described in this book. Perhaps this will result in another book at some point in the future.

Computing students often wonder why modules like project management and requirements analysis are part of their degree. The point of this book is to provide further support and more rationale for demonstrating the importance of business analysis and project management. I hope you found the book useful.

Appendix 1

Solutions

This appendix presents some solutions to the exercises set in the text.

Chapter 1. Business Concept Models

Exercise 1.

1. Rewrite business rules A1, A2.
   A1. A trade requires a specific number of items to trade.
   A2. A trade can only occur when a minimum value has been reached.

Note how unclear these business rules are now! They are too vague to be of use. We *need* the values for them to make sense.

2. The diagram of the revised A1 and A2:

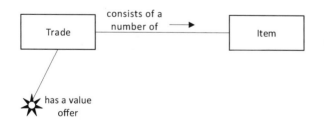

The same can be said for the diagram. The rules are open to interpretation in terms of the values. This version of the diagram offers opportunity for confusion rather than depicting business knowledge.

Exercise 2. Drop-off location.

1. Concept model diagram

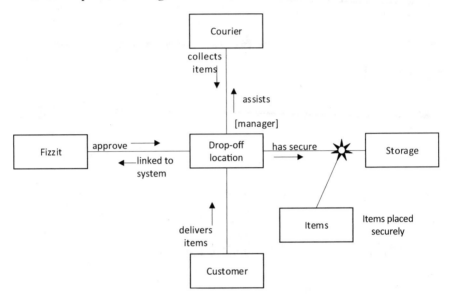

You will see in the diagram that Items are tagged to the line between drop-off location and storage. I wanted to make it clear that Items are vital in the business rules and so why not be very explicit about them? Hence, the sun-symbol indicating this is an active link when we associate the Items to it. You could have ignored this and simply had *items placed securely* on the line instead.

2. Definition of terms

Term	Definition	Example/Details
Item	A book, CD, DVD or computer console game (disc or cartridge version only).	Game consoles supported: Xbox 360 to current; PlayStation 3 to current.
Drop-off location	A storage facility where **customers** take their **items** for collection by Fizzit.	Examples: convenience stores (e.g. Martins), Tesco mini-store, Sainsbury mini-store. There are many other independent stores also acting as drop-off locations.
Customer	A person who is in the process of conducting a **trade**.	

Term	Definition	Example/Details
Storage	A secure area where **Customer items** are stored in a **drop-off location**	Examples are individual locker, secure storage room or shelving.
Courier	A collection service picking up **customer items** from **storage** in **drop-off locations** and delivering to the Fizzit warehouse.	The courier service is owned by Fizzit.
Fizzit system	The value chain created to conduct the business of Fizzit from end-to-end.	In this instance, Fizzit must ensure each drop-off location is connected to the Fizzit system to automatically inform Fizzit of arrival of items.

Note in the table I do not include Fizzit because it's very difficult to define the business that is the focus of this business concept model. In fact, the best advice is not to include businesses at all so you won't see TWOO defined either. Departments are different, so Courier gets defined here.

Chapter 2. BPMN

Exercise 1: Holiday booking.

The task asks to model a holiday process and the use of a voice recognition command system in a high-tech hotel. What I have done is my take on the process and I want to highlight some of the modelling techniques I have explained in the chapter. Here is the model. I will explain some of it once you've taken a look.

The process begins with the Holiday Maker booking an online holiday. Behind the scenes, the booking actually is made on an automated booking engine that books both the hotel and the flight. I've modelled these with databases, not hotel or airline pools. You could include pools but for us, we don't really worry about where the ticket or hotel booking is coming from. Many online travel agents buy up air tickets and rooms direct from airlines and hotels and we buy from them. I have demonstrated data a little superfluously because the Hotel action makes it clear it needs the booking record. There is a clock in the Holiday Maker pool. This signifies some time (as documented) has passed or can be used as a limiter: you can only do 'x' if 'y' occurs within e.g. 24 hours. In our case, we state: 'on date of travel' do something. That something is going on holiday. When in Beijing, in the hotel and in the room, the

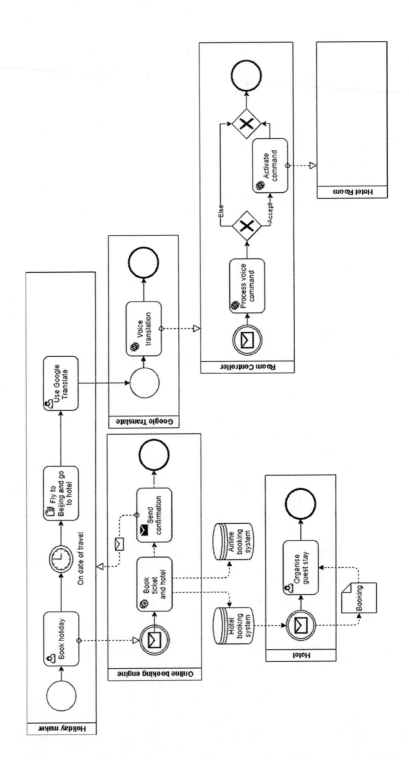

Holiday Maker uses Google Translate. This then broadcasts the translation. A Room Controller picks up the voice command and checks it understands it. If it doesn't, then the process ends here. The 'Else' is a catch all for anything the Controller does not understand. If the message makes sense then the Room Controller signals the relevant object in the room to obey the command. I don't model it like this but have an empty Hotel Room pool that receives the command at its edge. If your model is a little different, this is fine so long as you can explain it and the notation is used correctly.

Exercise 2: Fizzit drop-off location.

I originally thought this part of the process model would be straightforward for you to do. In a way, it is but I've added a different diagram

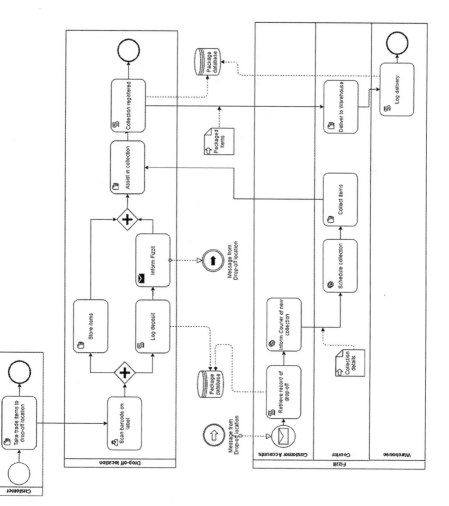

element you may not have seen. These are the two arrows in circles. The first arrow you need to consider is the darker one which is called a 'link throwing' event. This is used when you have an element in your process you wish to continue with later or elsewhere. I am using this to simply help fit the process model more easily on the page. I didn't really have to use it but choose to demonstrate it. The process continues with the 'link catching' event which is the lighter arrow in the circle. You read the process top-to-bottom until you get to the darker arrow. Then you need to search for the lighter arrow to recommence. Normally, these link-throwing and catching event arrows are used when an element in a process model has been active but does not need to do anything until much later. For example, an action in a pool whose next step is not required until much later in the process. You can link-throw and end the pool to then reintroduce it much later in the model. This means you don't have to drag the pool across several pages, for instance, with nothing happening in it.

I've kept the databases separate from pools because it's not certain who owns them. As this is a design of a to-be process, I won't assume ownership until the business partners confirm it.

The Fizzit pool, as you can see, has three swimlanes within it. I could have kept these all separate pools: Fizzit (replacing Customer Accounts), Courier and Warehouse. But as Customer Accounts might be the department within Fizzit managing the customer's records and transactions, I thought we should introduce it here. The Courier and Warehouse are also departments of Fizzit and as such are represented as swimlanes within the Fizzit pool. Note it is not permitted (according to the rules of BPMN) to send messages within the same pool from swimlane to swimlane. I've also included script event types but again I don't include the code because we are dealing with a business process. But by flagging that these actions need to be coded, we are giving the developers a heads up.

One last thing: if you look at the business concept model above (figure 2 and table in exercise 2 in this appendix) you can see the business concept model for the drop-off location. You'll find the business rules in chapter 1 and also in Appendix 2 showing the whole case study. I think we are a good match but the detail in the process model is much greater. However, the business knowledge blueprint gives us solid grounding in how to approach understanding the business problem. Finally, as ever, this model is my interpretation. Yours could be different but equally valid.

Chapter 3. Problem Frames

1. The Basic Workpiece should be straightforward for you to model given that it is already in the chapter, though wrapped within the

multiframe for Google Translate. I've stayed to the most basic view of the problem frame because it is best to begin with basics. My goal here has been only for you to identify what's relevant and what's not.

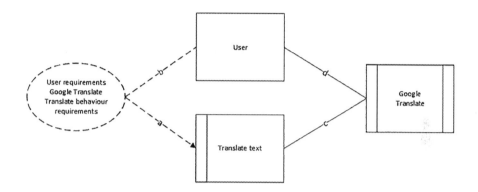

The requirements are given already in the chapter.

2. The Voice Controller is bit trickier. Here is my version of it, first pass. I've been a bit sneaky here and made it a Commanded Behaviour problem frame. You will see there are two machines. This is a reasonable assumption because Google Translate does not open the door or curtain. There's a different machine for that job. Google Translate simply broadcasts the voice command. This is picked up by another domain, the Voice Recognition Receiver that we would have to design. It is actually feasible to consider this a third machine domain. But let's not overdo it. This Voice Recognition Receiver domain could be a microphone at its most simplistic. A microphone of sorts would be deployed somewhere in the room and presumably it would be permanently 'on'. It's not in the machine domain because what needs to be there is a domain that can distinguish conversation, the television and a command for behaviour, sort out the noise and ignore that which isn't a command for action. So, we have the Room Controller machine domain. The bedroom has been expanded out to include its contents, or sub-domains. We can see, for example, the Room Controller has to signal the Door Lock if the voice command is 'open door' or 'lock door' or even 'unlock door'. I have decided to include the switch or lock or pulley in their respective domains because we are not commanding the door per se but its lock. We are not commanding the curtains change behaviour but the state of the electronic pulley to change from 'open' to 'close' for example.

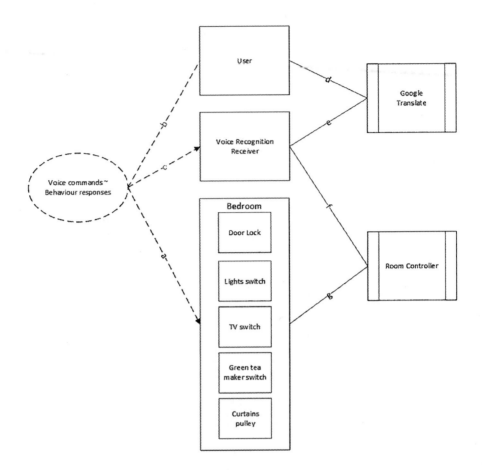

The requirements table shows that I've split the commanded behaviour into two, grouping requirements per machine (Google Translate and Room Controller). You don't have to but I think anything that helps keep a separation of concerns is worth doing. This can reduce design coupling where elements of design are unnecessarily linked. That's an object-oriented design principle but applies throughout the lifecycle for object-oriented, and indeed other, types of systems.

Problem Frame	Label	Description
Commanded Behaviour (Google Translate)	b	Input command words for voice
	c	Receive, recognise command words; ignore unrecognised words
	d	Recognise word; translate to Chinese
	e	Broadcast voice command word (in Chinese)

Problem Frame	Label	Description
Commanded Behaviour (Room Controller)	a	Open; close; on; off; identify correct device as broadcast in (e)
	f	Receive command
	g	Open/close/on/off correct device

Chapter 4. Requirements

1.

#	Requirement	Type
1	Deliver 15% performance improvement in output of products off production line.	Business
2	User must provide two forms of identification before process begins.	User
3	The light must change from red to green when 'Go' button is pressed.	Function
4	The change from red to green must occur within 0.5 seconds and remain green for a further 120 seconds.	Quality (time)
5	New product feature results in capturing 10% more market share.	Business
6	The system displays the customer booking prior to credit card payment as confirmation.	Function
7	If the user drops the phone on a hard surface from less than 2 meters, there should be no degradation of function or effect on the performance of the phone.	Quality (Robustness / Reliability)

2. Specification table for QA check (Fizzit)

ID	Requirement	Data	Process	Inputs	Outputs	Quality	Priority
FR1	The QA operator must correctly identify the package record	Package (trade) ID	See BPMN 'Fizzit QA & Payment' in Appendix 2.	Barcode on package (scanned or typed)	Trade ID, anonymous trade details	Trade record details 100% accurate 99.9% of time. Record retrieved within 10 seconds of scan 100% of time.	0 (MVP)

ID	Requirement	Data	Process	Inputs	Outputs	Quality	Priority
FR2	The QA operator must accurately record the quality of each item	Item barcode, quality rating (good, poor); rationale for poor (text)	See BPMN 'Fizzit QA & Payment' in Appendix 2.	Rating, rationale	Acknowledge input	N/A	0 (MPV)
FR2.1	Item identified as poor quality.	Customer account ID; three strikes rating	See BPMN 'Fizzit QA & Payment' in Appendix 2.	Item barcode; poor quality selected	For Customer Accounts Dept viewing only: strike rating raised; Customer account details	N/A	0 (MPV)
FR3	The QA operator must close a completed check before commencing a new package check.	Checked status (complete)	See BPMN 'Fizzit QA & Payment' in Appendix 2.	Select 'Check completed' (click)	For Customer Accounts Dept viewing only: Customer account updated	N/A	0 (MPV)

■ Requirements FR2.1 and FR3 outputs can only be viewed by the Customer Accounts Department, and not at all by the QA operator. Also note that I have changed the requirement ID numbers in Appendix 2 to fit with the other requirements for Fizzit.

Chapter 5. Use Cases

Use case diagram

High street bank system example.

Note the <<extends>> use case pointing into the exchange foreign currency use case. I think this is a flaw in the understanding of extension points because this behaviour isn't odd or unusual. Rather it is uncommon. There are several <<includes>> to access customer account use case. And finally, there is an actor within the system boundary representing the customer account record. I could have drawn this as a UML object. Or I could have left it out. Either way is fine. I just wanted to show you an example of usage.

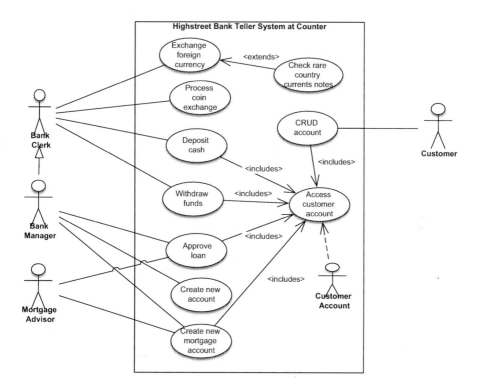

Use case description

UC1. Buy music

Actors: Customer, Member Customer

Trigger: Customer/Member Customer is logged in and has a valid account if Member Customer

Context: A Customer wants to buy music to download to complete their collection of Beethoven's concertos.

Pre-condition: Customer has a valid payment method. *Assumption that Customer cannot purchase unless becoming a member? Check business rules.*

Main Flow of Events:

1. Customer <u>searches catalogue</u> for music to purchase.
2. System displays customer search items.
3. Customer selects music to purchase.
4. System presents payment screen [see lo-fi prototype figure lfp.17]
5. Customer inputs payment details.
6. System approves payment.
7. Customer downloads purchased music.
8. End-use case.

Post-conditions: payment processed successfully, customer account updated, music downloaded successfully.

Alternative flow of events:

a5. Customer chooses saved payment method.

Exceptional flow of events:

e6. System rejects payment.
e6i. System informs Customer of rejected payment.
e6ii. Return to step 4 in main flow of events.

A note on the pre-condition – I have included an *assumption* here and it is not necessarily correct but something to be flagged. Do we want guest payments or must purchasers be members with accounts? This is a business rule issue and you will need to pass this up the hierarchy of management to find out, if it isn't clear. As an analyst, it is your job to analyse and raise questions. It's not good enough to just write down everything without further analysis of the appropriateness of the use case or requirement or any other aspect of the project you are responsible for. So please do raise questions, please do write down assumptions and make sure they are clarified. You will be doing your client a favour.

Something else: step 4 in the main flow has included a note: [see lo-fi prototype figure lfp.17]. If there are screens already in process of design or designed, then why not assist the developer – and even the customer – in linking to the specific screen for that step or steps in the use case?

Chapter 7. Product Breakdown Structure

PBS1.

The following is a potential solution to the question but this doesn't mean this is all there is. You might well have included far more detail than me. This is good but there's a risk and that is you put so much detail into this planning deliverable that the subsequent planning is made too complex. You might become too prescriptive or constrain the development too much.

1. Project Documentation

The main documents I recommend are a completed Requirements document. I call it a Requirements Specification but you could call

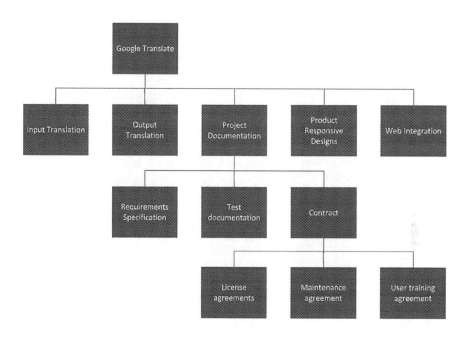

it: Requirements document, Specification, or whatever is appropriate in your situation. Right now, though, we'll call it a Requirements Specification. It lists the requirements to be built of which some could be more detailed in the form of a specification. I have also recommended that Test documentation be included formally. Testing is part of a project that often gets pushed aside until the last minute because deadlines are too tight. But by including it up-front, it ought to mean test plans are drawn up earlier than they otherwise might be and as such, the right amount of time will be allocated to the testing tasks. I have also included Contract here because without this, the project won't start. The sub-products of the Contract include any specific license agreements that may be needed – for instance for any specific tools embedded in the product, a maintenance agreement so the project team can prepare for life post-delivery. Finally, a user training agreement whenever users need to learn the product. This might include a user manual. For the Translate example, this might be going a bit too far but my experience is that project managers need to really get to grips with all the legal stuff pretty early on.

Chapter 8. Gantt Chart

Complete the Fizzit Gantt chart for Functional Requirement 1:

FR1. The Customer must create an account and log in before any other functions possible

FR1. The Customer must create an account and log in before any other functions possible	10 days	Mon 25/01/21	Fri 05/02/21	3,4,5
FR1.1. Screen designs	2 days	Mon 25/01/2:	Tue 26/01/21	
FR1.2. Database Tables	4 days	Wed 27/01/2:	Mon 01/02/2:	7
FR1.3. Security and privacy controls	4 days	Tue 02/02/21	Fri 05/02/21	8

The above solution is a suggestion. Though I have written about avoiding bland statements, I go and use them in FR1.1 and FR1.2! If I were being completely honest, I might not bother to list FR1.1 simply because a log-in screen is very standard. Developers simply know how to do it. However, we do need to capture customer details when they register and this could include financial details – where should Fizzit send payment to? As such, the database programmer needs to consider how to store such data, hence FR1.2. The final line item, FR1.3 Security and privacy controls, are important to implement because Fizzit will be storing very sensitive data and must ensure confidentiality, integrity, authentication and availability.

You'll notice the layout of the chart as a stepdown from one task to the next. There is no notion of parallel work occurring. Why is this? It is because we are assuming that only one developer is taking on this function. We can ask if this is reasonable. I suggest it is probably not. You would have a specialist database programmer and a specialist interface designer and even a specialist cybersecurity developer. If this were the case, then there would be overlap in each or some of the tasks. I present the figure as it shows some variety compared to the larger Gantt chart, which you can see in Appendix 2.

Chapter 9. Kanban

Create a Kanban board for FR1 – the same requirement as in the Gantt chart exercise above. You'll note there are only three tasks documented in the Gantt chart. We are asked to put the board together from Specify Active to Implement Active. That is three columns.

This is a very basic requirement. More complex boards are created with more complex requirements. Appendix 2 provides a detailed Kanban board for the Fizzit case.

Appendix 2

Fizzit.com Case Study

Business Rules

A. Trade Rules

A1. A trade can only occur when there is between a minimum of 10 items and a maximum of 99 to be traded.

A2. A trade can only occur when a value offered of £10 is reached.

A3. A trade cannot occur if 10 items are presented but the value is below £10.

A4. Fizzit pays Customer on completion of the trade the completed trade value amount.

A5. A trade must request a drop-off location.

A6. A trade cannot be cancelled once items are stored at a drop-off location.

A7. A trade must include the Customer's bank account sort code and account number or PayPal address.

A8. An item for a trade can only be identified by its barcode or ISBN.

A9. The price offered for an item is determined by TWOO plus an additional 5 per cent markup for Fizzit.

B. Drop-Off Location Rules

B1. The drop-off location must be approved by Fizzit.

B2. The drop-off location must directly link to Fizzit's system.

B3. The drop-off location must provide adequate storage to hold the Customer's items.

B4. The drop-off location must inform Fizzit of the arrival of the Customer's items.

B5. The drop-off location manager should assist the courier in collecting the Customer's items.

C. Couriers Rules

C1. Fizzit couriers collect Customer items from drop-off locations and deliver items to the Fizzit Warehouse.

C2. Couriers must notify Fizzit of a successful pick up at the point of pick up, the drop-off location.

D. Quality Assurance (QA) Rules

D1. A QA operator in the Fizzit Warehouse inspects Customer items for damage that if found renders the item unsellable.

D2. Items not found in the Trade record must not be traded.

D3. Extra items found in the Customer items must not be traded.

D4. All extra items will be recycled (see G. RECYCLING RULES).

D5. All non-approved items must be recycled.

D6. All non-damaged items are approved for the trade.

D7. A QA operator's decision on product quality is final.

D8. A QA check on a Trade is only complete when all Customer items have been reviewed and each item is approved or rejected as damaged.

D9. A Customer's items must be assessed for quality within 24 hours of arrival at warehouse.

D10. Fizzit must provide explicit instructions on how to review items: what is acceptable and what is not. [Acceptance is variable over time – updates are kept in the Definition of Terms.]

E. Accounts Rules

E1. Accounts must authorise Customer payment.

E2. Accounts must only pay the Customer the amount of the total of approved item offer prices.

E3. In all transactions, a copy of the transaction is given to the Customer.

E4. The Customer must be paid within 24 hours of completion of the QA process.

F. TWOO Rules

F1. TWOO sends weekly updates to Fizzit on trending products.

F2. If an item sells within 24 hours of going onto the TWOO site more than 10 times in a row, then Fizzit are instructed to offer Customers 10 per cent more for that item.

F3. If an item sells within 48 hours of going onto the TWOO site more than 10 times in a row, then Fizzit are instructed to offer Customers 5 per cent more for that item.

F4. If an item does not sell within five working days of going onto the TWOO site, Fizzit will refuse this item when a Customer offers it until F2 or F3 occur again.

F5. TWOO has the right to change the frequencies, schedules and percentages as listed in F2, F3, F4 at their discretion.

G. Recycling Rules

G1. All items designated as damaged are recycled in their entirety.

G2. Recycling must occur within a 5-mile radius of the Warehouse to ensure minimal transport costs (environmental as well as financial).

G3. Fizzit encourages Customers to recycle their own damaged items.

G4. Customers can receive a 12-month ban from trading when three-or-more damaged items are received in a trade.

G5. Rule G4 is subject to management decision upon reviewing the Customer's trading history.

H. Customer Rules

H1. A Customer is anyone who registers with the Fizzit website.

H2. A Customer can:
- Conduct a trade
- Reserve items to be traded later (see technical requirements document)
- Stop a trade from occurring at any point prior to taking items to a drop-off location.

H3. A Customer cannot:
- Stop a trade after items have been registered at a drop-off location
- Change bank account details when a trade is in process
- Ask for items back unless exceptional circumstances permit this [these exceptions must be agreed by the business].

H4. When a Customer accepts a trade offer value, the offer remains at this value until the trade is completed or cancelled.

H5. A Customer cannot conduct a trade unless registered.

H6. A registration is incomplete unless bank account and/or PayPal information is included.

H7. A registration does not need to be completed until the point at which a Customer wants to submit a trade.

Concept Model Diagram

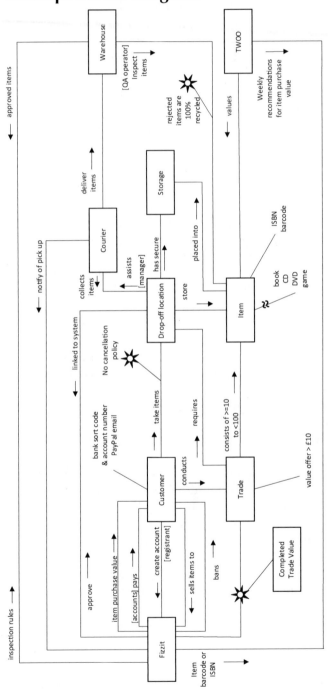

Fizzit Definition of Terms

Term	Definition	Example/Details
Trade	Act or process of buying or selling **items**.	
Item	A book, CD, DVD or computer console game (disc or cartridge version only).	Game consoles supported: Xbox 360 to current; PlayStation 3 to current.
Drop-off location	A storage facility where **customers** take their **items** for collection by Fizzit.	Examples: convenience stores (e.g. Martins), Tesco mini-store, Sainsbury mini-store. There are many other independent stores also acting as drop-off locations.
Customer	A person who is in the process of conducting a **trade**.	
Registrant	A person who has completed the Fizzit online registration. A registrant has not started the process of a **trade**. A registrant has never conducted a trade.	A registrant who commences a **trade** for the first time is designated as a **Customer** (and is no longer a registrant).
Storage	A secure area where **Customer items** are stored in a **drop-off location**	Examples are: individual locker, secure storage room or shelving.
Courier	A collection service picking up **customer items** from **storage** in **drop-off locations** and delivering to the Fizzit warehouse.	The courier service is owned by Fizzit.
Fizzit system	The value chain created to conduct the business of Fizzit from end-to-end.	Example parts of the value chain are: Customer and customer trade, courier, drop-off location, quality control, TWOO.
Damaged book	Not in good enough condition to sell easily on TWOO	Current list of damage causing quality inspection (QA) to fail: missing page(s), torn off page piece(s), scribbling/writing on text on page obscuring text or image, broken spine, split spine, cover torn rendering it non-protective.

(Continued)

Term	Definition	Example/Details
Damaged CD or DVD or game	Item and packaging not in good enough condition to sell easily on TWOO	Current list of damage causing QA fail: clearly identifiable pirate/fake copy, scratches on disc, insert missing, insert torn, insert written/scribbled on; broken case [cannot close], spine of case broken
Accounts	Department within Fizzit responsible for managing **Customer** payments.	
Offer price	The amount of money (in Sterling) that TWOO offers to pay for each **item** the **Customer** wishes to sell.	The Customer wants to sell her copy of *Harry Potter and the Philosopher's Stone*; an offer price will be made by TWOO to purchase this book, if and only if TWOO wants to on-sell the book.
Transaction	Payment made by **Accounts** to a **Customer** (the amount of the **trade** minus the value of the offer made on **damaged items**).	Fizzit offers a Customer a total trade offer value of £17.58 for 13 books. Upon QA inspection, one book is found to be damaged. Fizzit's offer value for this item was £1.12. This amount is subtracted from the original trade offer value: £17.58 - £1.12 = £16.46. The Customer is paid £16.46 in the transaction.
Customer payment	Funds transferred from Fizzit to the **Customer's** account.	
'Recycled in their entirety'	No part of an **item** is left unrecycled. Recycled: to pass through or undergo again, as for further treatment, change, use, etc.	A CD comes with a case, paper-based insert(s), and a disc. All of which are 100% recycled or reused.

Fizzit Business Process Models

Note: 'Customer trade' process, 'Add item to trade' and 'Complete trade' subprocesses are presented in Chapter 2.

Drop-Off Location Process

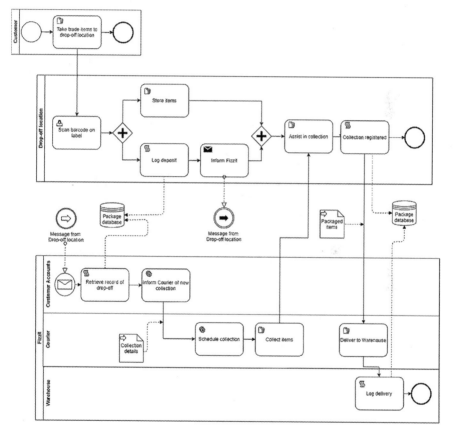

Fizzit QA and Payment

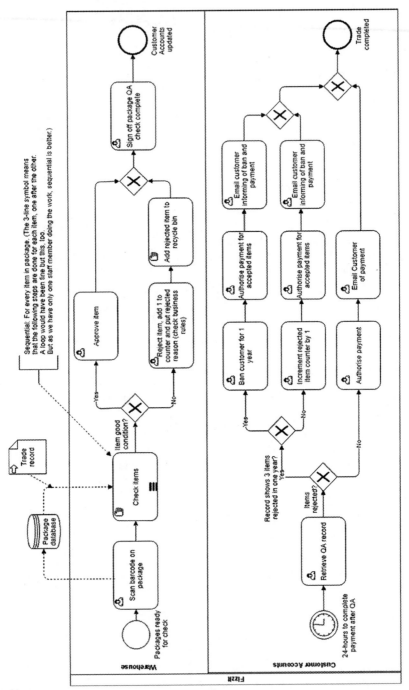

Note I have not included the Customer or their payment organisation here (e.g. PayPal). If I were to, they would be separate pools and I would send a message from the edge of the Fizzit pool to each. I would not show several messages coming from inside the Customer Accounts swimlane because there are three potential messages to pay and three to email, too many to model without making a mess. I would not model any communications between the payment provider and the Customer as this is out of scope of Fizzit's business.

I put a timer on the start of the Customer Accounts process because they have 24 hours to pay once the QA process is complete (business rule E4).

Problem Frames

Customer Trade (Workpiece and Required Behaviour frames)

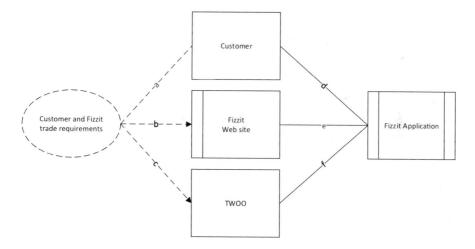

I don't have the Fizzit website as the machine domain because what we are really seeing is a shop front. The engine behind that shop front is the whole Fizzit Application. We do denote the Fizzit Website as a design domain – the single stripe – because we do have to design it. This is a multi-frame problem. The Fizzit Application must behave according to the requirements but allow the Customer flexibility to make decisions on trading items. At its most basic, this is form filling, so a Workpiece. TWOO, on the other hand, is required to behave according to the requirements. There's no human commanding TWOO; it is indirect. We can think of TWOO as a system we need to interact with. What is direct is the message from the Fizzit application. So TWOO must respond, or is required to respond, appropriately.

Drop-Off Location (Workpiece)

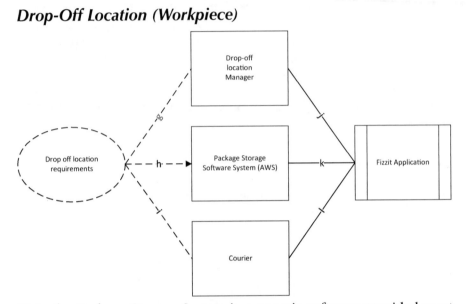

Note the Package Storage System is a generic software provided most often by Amazon Web Services (AWS). It isn't bespoke to Fizzit because there are a growing number of businesses in need of such a system. As such, it is not a design domain (though it remains Causal) because Fizzit may only need it tailored to the Fizzit brand. Or it may simply come out of the box and there's nothing Fizzit can do to alter it. The AWS is primarily viewed as a form by both the employee and Courier. It is therefore a Workpiece, a spreadsheet frontend. We are not concerned with anything more than it connects to the Fizzit Application.

QA Check (Workpiece)

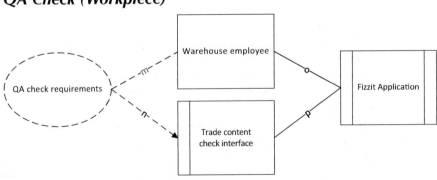

Customer Payment (Commanded Behaviour)

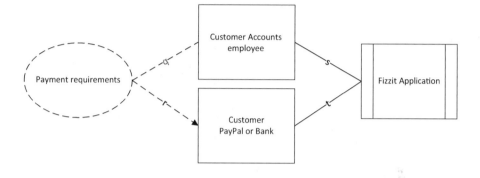

Requirements

Note I did not create one multiframe problem that encompasses all the problem frames because I think there needs to be more separation of concerns with this system. You could combine everything as the Fizzit Application is the machine domain but I don't believe a multi-frame problem frame adds anything to our understanding. Note that the requirements are effectively just notes to give a broader understanding of the problem frames and the required system responses. We could go into much more detail on requirements and even semi-formalise them according optative and indicative behaviours on domains. This is Jackson's full problem frames approach. I think for us, we can explore these areas in much more detail some other time. For now, it is not so important to do so. We are at the crossroads of business modelling and requirements modelling.

Problem Frame	Label	Description
Customer Trade	a	Input barcodes/ISBN; input account details
(Workpiece and	b	Display Customer input and response
Required Behaviour)	c	Return book value
	d	Acknowledge; accept/reject input
	e	Correct response and screen display
	f	Send book ISBN/barcode; receive book value
Drop-off Location	g	Process customer package correctly
(Workpiece)	h	Display Manager input and response
	i	Pick up package
	j	Acknowledge; accept/reject input
	k	Correct response and screen display
	l	Location, package, schedule

(Continued)

Problem Frame	Label	Description
QA Check (Workpiece)	m	Process customer items correctly
	n	Represent customer items and QA employee inputs correctly
	o	Acknowledge; accept/reject input
	p	Correct response and screen display
Customer Payment	q	Pay customer
(Commanded Behaviour)	r	Authorise payment
	s	Identify correct customer trade record
	t	Funds transfer

Requirements Specification Tables

Conducting a trade (Customer view)

ID	Requirement	Data	Process	Inputs	Outputs	Quality	Priority
FR1	The Customer must create an account and log in before any other function is possible	Customer email; encrypted password; Customer details: name, address, [bank sort code and account number can be captured but not initially needed]	See BPMN 'Customer Trade Process'	[See data]	Acknowledge account created	N/A	0 (MVP)
FR2	Each item must return a price value	Item barcode; price value	See BPMN 'Add item to trade subprocess'	Item barcode	Price value [can be 0 i.e. not wanted]	TWOO must return result within 5 seconds	0 (MVP)
FR3	Customer can add item with a >0 price value to a trade	Item barcode; price value; total trade value	See BPMN 'Add item to trade subprocess'	Place item in trade list*	Non-trade list updated. Trade list updated with new item; total trade amount updated.	N/A	0 (MPV)

(*Continued*)

ID	Requirement	Data	Process	Inputs	Outputs	Quality	Priority
FR4	Customer can remove item from a trade	Item barcode; price value; total trade value	N/A	Remove item selected	Trade list updated with new item; total trade amount updated. Non-trade list updated.	N/A	1 (Should)
FR5	System informs when trade permitted	Number of items >= 10; total trade value >= £10	See BPMN 'Complete trade subprocess'	[See data - Count of items and value]	Inform customer message	N/A	0 (MVP)
FR6	Customer can save items for later trade	Item barcodes; price value [holds for 14 calendar days from first price value return FR2]	See BPMN 'Add item to trade subprocess'	[See data] Place item in 'save for later' list	Acknowledge	N/A	2 (Could)
FR6.1	Upon Customer log in any 'save for later' items must still be visible	Item barcodes; price value [holds for 14 calendar days]	See FR6	Customer logged in	View list	N/A	0 (MVP) [Note only if FR6 is built then FR6.1 must be built.]
FR7	Customer conducts trade [subject to enough items and value to be traded]	Item barcodes; total trade value; customer account ID; payment details required: bank sort code and account number or Paypal email	See BPMN 'Complete trade subprocess'	Trade selected [items >= 10; value >= £10]	Trade acknowledged; trade UID generated; email sent to customer; customer account updated	Conducted securely	0 (MVP)

* Note that I am not saying anything about the appearance of the Fizzit application at all. I leave this to the UXD and other design specialists to best work it out.

Drop-Off Location

ID	Requirement	Data	Process	Inputs	Outputs	Quality	Priority
FR8	The drop-off location clerk (clerk from here on in) scans package barcode	Package barcode; date; time; location ID	See BPMN 'drop-off location process'	Package barcode (scanned)	Acknowledge; print receipt; identify storage box/location for package; Fizzit informed	N/A	0 (MVP)
FR9	Courier collects package	Location ID; courier ID; package ID; date; time	See BPMN 'drop-off location process'	[See data]	Acknowledge package collected; Fizzit informed	N/A	0 (MPV)
FR10	Package delivered to Fizzit warehouse	Courier ID; package ID; date; time	See BPMN 'drop-off location process'	[See data]	Acknowledge package delivered; Fizzit Customer Accounts Dept informed; Customer informed (email)	N/A	0 (MPV)

Quality Assurance Check

ID	Requirement	Data	Process	Inputs	Outputs	Quality	Priority
FR11	The QA operator must correctly identify the package record	Package (trade) ID	See BPMN 'Fizzit QA & Payment' in Appendix 2.	Barcode on package (scanned or typed)	Trade ID, anonymous trade details	Trade record details 100% accurate 99.9% of time. Record retrieved within 10 seconds of scan 100% of time.	0 (MVP)
FR12	The QA operator must accurately record the quality of each item	Item barcode, quality rating (good, poor); rationale for poor (text)	See BPMN 'Fizzit QA & Payment' in Appendix 2.	Rating, rationale	Acknowledge input	N/A	0 (MPV)
FR12.1	Item identified as poor quality.	Customer account ID; three strikes rating	See BPMN 'Fizzit QA & Payment' in Appendix 2.	Item barcode; poor quality selected	For Customer Accounts Dept viewing only: strike rating raised; Customer account details	N/A	0 (MPV)
FR13	The QA operator must close a completed check before commencing a new package check.	Checked status (complete)	See BPMN 'Fizzit QA & Payment' in Appendix 2.	Select 'Check completed' (click)	For Customer Accounts Dept viewing only: Customer account updated	N/A	0 (MPV)

Customer Payment

ID	Requirement	Data	Process	Inputs	Outputs	Quality	Priority
FR14	Customer Accounts pays customer trade value	Customer account; bank/ Paypal details; trade ID; total trade value	See BPMN 'Fizzit QA and payment'	QA trade complete	Monetary amount transferred to customer; email customer; updated accounts	Payment within 24 hours of QA check	0 (MVP)
FR15	[IF] Customer three strikes record [unsellable item - poor quality] incremented	Customer ID; strikes total; date; time	See BPMN 'Fizzit QA and payment'				1 (Should)
FR16	[IF FR15 activated] Strikes remain < 3 within one calendar year	Customer ID; strikes total; date; time	See BPMN 'Fizzit QA and payment'	[See data]	Customer informed (email)	N/A	0 (MVP)
FR17	[IF FR15 activated] Strikes now = 3 within one calendar year	Customer ID; strikes total; date; time	See BPMN 'Fizzit QA and payment'	[See data]	Customer informed (email); customer account frozen for one calendar year	Ensure account remains frozen for no more than one calendar year	0 (MVP)

Use Cases

Use Case Diagram

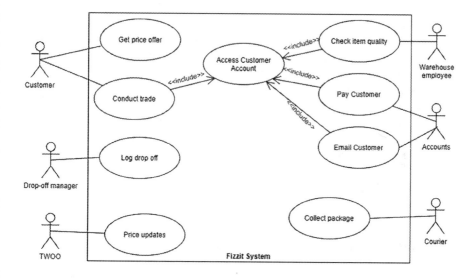

Note that the diagram represents external behaviour/functionality at the interfaces of the Fizzit System. I don't include Fizzit as an actor because it is Fizzit that is represented by the system. If anyone from Fizzit needed to use the system, that person would be an actor with an appropriate role name. In this case, we have Warehouse employee, Accounts, Courier. They line up on the right and this is deliberate to indicate they are an employee of Fizzit. The left side contains actors that may not be classified as being employed by Fizzit. A Customer could also be an employee but for clarity of roles, we do not have an individual who is both at the same time. There are four <<include>> stereotype relationships in the diagram, all to the use case Access Customer Account. The idea here is that: a trade cannot occur without knowing who is conducting the trade – an account is needed; it isn't possible to conduct the item QA check without a record of the trade items, accessed within the Customer account; and the Accounts actor cannot pay or email the Customer without knowing who to pay or email. To do this, the Accounts actor must access the Customer's account. I did not include Paypal or the Bank as actors because they are passive in that they receive only. Payment linkage is dealt with outside of this use case diagram but is flagged here as a use case as it is an important function of the process. The Accounts department has to also email the Customer with feedback on the trade, any warnings or a ban, plus include payment updates. I felt these two use cases, Pay Customer and Email Customer, needed some separation of concerns to avoid over-coupling them. Drop-off manager, TWOO and the Courier are included as these are important functions for the business model to succeed. No <<extend>> use cases are needed. I did think about it with regards to the rejection of item quality and even TWOO's rejection of the item for purchase, but I think rejection is not the same as error. Rejection of items isn't an error in the behaviour of an actor in a process or on the system. We have nine use cases in total and though this is small, it is enough to be getting on with. I did not include use cases such as create account. These are givens in modern-day web applications so to include such here would be stating the obvious. Though you're taught to be thorough, over-stating the use cases can be seen as naive. That said, it is quite normal to revise the use cases, add to the diagram and delete from the diagram as more is known about the actors and the solution options.

Use Case Descriptions

UC1. Get Price Offer

Actor: Customer

Trigger: Customer is ready with book/CDs/DVDs/games to trade.

Context: Customer has several old books that are no longer needed. Fizzit appears to be a way for someone else to read them and to earn a small amount in the process.

Pre-conditions: Customer is logged in. Fizzit application is on input screen.

Main Flow of Events:

1. Customer inputs item ISBN/barcode.
2. System presents price offer information.
3. Customer adds item to 'trade'.

End-use case

Post-conditions: trade value incremented by price offer amount.

Alternative flow of events:

a2. System rejects item.

End-use case

Alternative flow of events:

a3. Customer rejects price offer

Alternative flow of events:

a3. Customer places item in 'save for later'

UC2. Conduct Trade

Actor: Customer
Trigger: [Context and pre-conditions sufficient]
Context: The Customer has inputted items to be traded.
Pre-conditions: Customer logged in, account completed, value of
    trade > £10 and number of items in trade > 10
Main flow of events:

1. Customer chooses conduct trade.
2. System displays items to trade.
3. Customer confirms items to trade.
4. System presents drop-off location options.
5. Customer selects drop-off location.
6. System <u>accesses Customer account</u> to confirm payment type.
7. Customer selects payment type [PayPal or bank account transfer].
8. System asks Customer to confirm trade.
9. Customer confirms trade.
10. System acknowledges trade now in progress.

End-use case.

Post-condition: trade submitted for processing.

Alternative flow of events:

a3. Customer refuses to start trade.

End-use case.

Alternative flow of events:

a6. System <u>accesses Customer account</u> to confirm payment type.
a6i. System asks for payment type to be input.
a6ii. Customer inputs payment type [PayPal or bank account transfer]
a6iii. Return to main flow step 7.

Alternative flow of events:

a9. Customer refuses to start trade.

End-use case.

UC3. Log Drop-Off

Customer: Drop-off location manager
Trigger: Package contains scannable barcode. Package is acceptably
sealed.
Context: Customer brings package to drop-off location.
Pre-conditions: Drop-off system [subsystem of Fizzit application]
interface open. Manager logged in.
Main flow of events:

1. Manager scans package barcode.
2. System acknowledges valid barcode.
3. System opens locker door.

End-use case.

Post-conditions: Fizzit informed of successful drop-off.

Alternative flow of events:

a2. System rejects barcode scan.
a2i. Manager inputs barcode on keyboard.
a2ii. Return to step 2 in main flow.

Exceptional flow of events:

e2. System rejects barcode scan.
e2i. Manager inputs barcode on keyboard.
e2ii. System rejects barcode.
e2iii. System rejects package.

Assumption for exceptional flow is there is a manual workaround.
TBD.

UC4. Price Updates

Actor: TWOO (machine/system actor)
Trigger: Every seven days, TWOO has revised prices for items.
Context: To keep customers engaged, TWOO offers more for popu-
lar items so needs to inform Fizzit what current prices are. It is
expected this is an automated process.
Pre-condition: Seven days passed. Correct figures available.
Main flow of events:

1. TWOO accesses Fizzit price database.
2. TWOO updates prices.

End-use case.

Exceptional flow of events:

e1. TWOO unable to connect to Fizzit.
e1i. TWOO retries until successful.
e1ii. Return to main flow step 2.

Note that this use case has only two steps. It is questionable, therefore, whether we should include it as a use case. I personally might be tempted to drop it but not until I can confirm this later. Given that keeping prices up-to-date is a big deal in promoting this system – and business – it would be wise to include it so this key function does not get lost.

UC5. Check Item Quality

Actor: Warehouse employee
Trigger: Package has arrived at warehouse. 24 hours to complete inspection started [business rule D9].
Context: Each package, delivered by the Courier, must be checked for condition of items. The warehouse employee has unpackaged the items ready for inspection.
Pre-conditions: Warehouse employee logged into Fizzit system.
Main flow of events:

1. Warehouse employee scans barcode package.
2. System accesses Customer account to display items for trade.
3. Warehouse employee inputs quality of each item.
4. System acknowledges input.
5. Warehouse employee completes inspection.
6. System acknowledges inspection complete.

End-use case.

Post-condition: System ready for next inspection. Customer account updated.

Alternative flow of events:

a2. System unable to accesses Customer account.
a2i. Warehouse employee manually inputs package barcode.
a2ii. Return to main flow step 2.

Exceptional flow of events:

e2. System unable to find customer account.
e2i. Warehouse employee informs manager.

End-use case.

Assumption is that requirements will make it clear what happens to items of good quality vs poor quality – note business rules section D.

UC6. Pay Customer

Actor: Accounts
Trigger: Accounts department employee informed of completed inspection.
Context: Customer must be paid with 24 hours of completed inspection [business rule E4].
Pre-condition: Inspection complete. Correct payment amount calculated. Accounts employee logged in and has approval to authorise payment. Payment gateway open.
Main flow of events:

1. Accounts employee <u>accesses customer account</u>.
2. System acknowledges customer reference.
3. Accounts selects payment type.
4. System acknowledges payment type.
5. Accounts inputs payment amount.
6. System confirms amount.
7. Accounts pays customer.
8. System confirms payment made.

End-use case.

Post-conditions: Payment completed, customer account updated.

Exceptional flow of events:

e8. Payment fails.
e8i. Return to main flow step 1.

Assumption of a manual workaround if repeated failure to process payment. TBD.

UC7. Email Customer

Actor: Accounts
Trigger: [see context and pre-conditions]
Context: Once payment has been processed, Fizzit informs the customer of the output of the inspection.
Pre-condition: Payment process is complete.
Main flow of events:

1. Accounts employee <u>accesses customer account</u>.
2. System acknowledges customer reference.
3. Accounts completes email message.
4. System sends message.

End-use case.

Post-conditions: Customer account updated [email acknowledgement, payment amount, items purchased by Fizzit, items rejected by Fizzit and reason, current status of customer account (active, active with warning, blocked)]

Exceptional flow of events:

e4. Email send fails.
e4i. Return to main flow step 3.

Assumption of a manual workaround if repeated failure to process email. TBD.

UC8. Collect Package

Actor: Courier
Trigger: Logged package at drop-off location
Context: Once every day, couriers go to drop-off locations collect packages and deliver them to the warehouse for inspection.
Pre-condition: Courier logged into Fizzit system.
Main flow of events:

1. System informs Courier of new collection.
2. Courier acknowledges message.
3. Courier confirms pick up from drop-off location.

Use case end.

Post-condition: Package on-route or at warehouse.
Exceptional flow of events:

e3. Package not at warehouse.
e3i. Courier informs Fizzit.

End-use case.

Note there is a break in the use case writing rules here because we have the Courier doing two things in a row. Local coherence is not present. The rules are there to be used but sometimes the situation dictates a 'bending' of them. This is one such situation because in effect, step 3 is all by itself one function and not really a use case step. Again, I have included it here to make sure we have a better understanding of the requirements. We could simply remove this entire use case from the model but we would still need to include it in the requirements. I keep it here for now. As we progress on the project, we might decide to remove it.

UC9: Access Customer Account <<include>>

Actors: Customer, Warehouse Employee, Accounts
Trigger: Actors access this <<include>> use case from their respective use cases: UC2, UC5, UC6, UC7.
Context: in order for UC2, UC5, UC6, UC7 to work, a customer account must have been completed.
Pre-conditions: See trigger
Main flow of events:

1. Actor requests account.
2. System displays account.

Exceptional flow of events:

e2. Account not found.

End-use case.

Note this use case helps actors complete their tasks. The customer filling out an account form isn't interesting enough to include as a use case. But the fact that four use cases need to access that account to be successful is. So we should <<include>> it.

Product Breakdown Structure

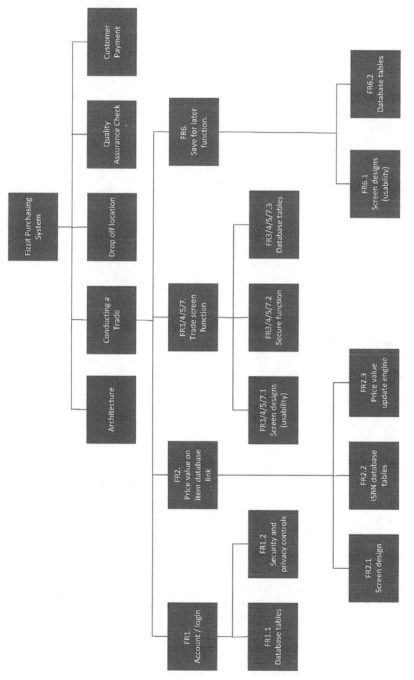

Note the PBS is only a partial model – it addresses only the first main theme, 'Conducting a Trade'. It also only includes those products that we really need to think more deeply about. Run-of-the-mill products tend not to be included because a development team should be experienced enough to know what to produce from the requirements documentation as well as the PBS.

Gantt Chart

Note there are four images required to be able to display the Gantt chart for the product breakdown structure documented immediately above. The tool used for the Gantt chart is Microsoft Project, used with permission from Microsoft.

	Task Name	Duration	Start	Finish	Predt	Resource Names	11 Jan '21	18 Jan '21	25 Jan '21
1	◢ Feasibility Study	10 days	Mon 11/01/2	Fri 22/01/21					
2	Business case	3 days	Mon 11/01/2	Wed 13/01/2		BA	BA		
3	Proof of concept	10 days	Mon 11/01/2	Fri 22/01/21		PM			PM
4	Clarify requirements	7 days	Thu 14/01/21	Fri 22/01/21		Arch			Arch
5	Build and test architecture	7 days	Thu 14/01/21	Fri 22/01/21					
6	◢ FR1. The Customer must create an account and log in before any other functions possible	10 days	Mon 25/01/21	Fri 05/02/21	3,4,5				
7	FR1.1. Screen designs	2 days	Mon 25/01/2	Tue 26/01/21		UXD			UXD
8	FR1.2. Database Tables	4 days	Wed 27/01/2	Mon 01/02/2	7	DBA			
9	FR1.3. Security and privacy controls	4 days	Tue 02/02/21	Fri 05/02/21	8	Dev			
10	◢ FR2.Each item must return a price value	10 days	Mon 25/01/2	Fri 05/02/21	5				
11	FR2.1. Screen designs	2 days	Mon 25/01/2	Tue 26/01/21		UXD			UXD
12	FR2.2 ISBN Database tables	5 days	Mon 25/01/2	Fri 29/01/21		DBA			
13	FR2.3 Price value update engine	10 days	Mon 25/01/2	Fri 05/02/21		Dev			
14	◢ FR3. Customer can add item with a >0 price value to a trade	5 days?	Mon 01/02/21	Fri 05/02/21					
15	FR3.1. Usability screen designs	2 days	Mon 01/02/2	Tue 02/02/2		UXD			
16	FR3.2. Secure function	5 days	Mon 01/02/2	Fri 05/02/21		Dev			
17	FR3.3. Database tables	4 days	Mon 01/02/2	Thu 04/02/2		DBA			
18	◢ FR4. Customer can remove item from a trade	5 days	Mon 08/02/2	Fri 12/02/21	6,10,14				
19	FR4.1. Usability screen designs	2 days	Mon 08/02/2	Tue 09/02/2		UXD			
20	FR4.2. Secure function	5 days	Mon 08/02/2	Fri 12/02/21		Dev			
21	FR4.3. Database tables	4 days	Mon 08/02/2	Thu 11/02/2		DBA			
22	◢ FR5. System informs when trade permitted	5 days	Mon 08/02/2	Fri 12/02/21					
23	FR5.1. Usability screen designs	2 days	Mon 08/02/2	Tue 09/02/2		UXD			

The above image is the first part of the Gantt chart. It focuses initially on the Feasibility study. The left side shows the requirements broken into tasks. Durations, dates, dependencies and resources are included. The right side shows the bar chart view. As you can see, we quickly go off the page. This is the one big weakness of the Gantt chart if not viewed on paper – it disappears off the screen. We could remove the weekend from the schedule and we could group into week blocks but this is a fairly short project so we need to know what is planned on a daily basis.

As you go through the below Gantt images you will notice similarity in FR3, 4, 5 and 7. These are all planned to occur in parallel and with the same staff. As I said, this is a plan so it will be easy for the plan to go wrong very quickly. Keeping the whole Gantt chart up-to-date is a significant weakness of the approach even if only one thing changes because of the knock-on effect, or ripple effect, through the remainder of the plan. It is just about inevitable that it will change, too. Other than this, the tool itself is a brilliant way to display the wider project view.

Kanban Board

Note that the following is a snapshot – a moment in the time of the project. There would be much more to include in the actual full-blown project but this gives you an idea. I only go as far as Implement Done here. Validation is yet to happen.

Backlog	Specify Active	Specify Done	Implement Active	Implement Done
FR5. System informs user when trade permitted	FR4. Customer can remove item from a trade	FR3.1. Usability screen designs	FR2.1. Screen Designs	FR1.1. Screen designs
FR6. Customer can save items for later trade	+ Add another card	FR3.2. Secure function	FR2.2. ISBN database tables	FR1.2. Database tables
FR7. Customer conducts trade [subject to enough items and value to be traded]		FR3.3. Database tables	FR2.3. Price value update engine	FR1.3. Security and privacy controls
+ Add another card		DONE RULES:	+ Add another card	DONE RULES:
		+ Add another card		+ Add another card

I have not included resource allocation in the Kanban board, just listing the tasks as they move across the board. Note how contrasting this 'simple' Kanban board appears to be compared to the Gantt chart above. Yet, Kanban is an ideal tool much more suited to developers when it comes to the detailed development work. Management of work items appears simpler. The Gantt chart's strength is in presenting the overall picture of the project end-to-end, or start-to-finish, which the Kanban board does not do easily.

Index

[Page numbers in *italics* denote figures, those in **bold** denote tables, and n denotes a note]